The

ARTIST'S WAY
EVERY DAY

BY JULIA CAMERON

The
ARTIST'S WAY EVERY DAY

· *A Year of Creative Living* ·

JULIA CAMERON

JEREMY P. TARCHER/PENGUIN
a member of Penguin Group (USA) Inc.
New York

JEREMY P. TARCHER/PENGUIN
Published by the Penguin Group
Penguin Group (USA) Inc., 375 Hudson Street, New York, New York 10014,
USA • Penguin Group (Canada), 90 Eglinton Avenue East, Suite 700, Toronto, Ontario
M4P 2Y3, Canada (a division of Pearson Canada Inc.) • Penguin Books Ltd,
80 Strand, London WC2R 0RL, England • Penguin Ireland, 25 St Stephen's Green,
Dublin 2, Ireland (a division of Penguin Books Ltd) • Penguin Group (Australia),
250 Camberwell Road, Camberwell, Victoria 3124, Australia (a division of Pearson
Australia Group Pty Ltd) • Penguin Books India Pvt Ltd, 11 Community Centre,
Panchsheel Park, New Delhi–110 017, India • Penguin Group (NZ), 67 Apollo Drive,
Rosedale, North Shore 0632, New Zealand (a division of Pearson
New Zealand Ltd) • Penguin Books (South Africa) (Pty) Ltd, 24 Sturdee Avenue,
Rosebank, Johannesburg 2196, South Africa

Penguin Books Ltd, Registered Offices: 80 Strand, London WC2R 0RL, England

Contains quotations from *The Artist's Way*,
Walking in This World, Finding Water, The Sound of Paper, The Right to Write,
and *The Vein of Gold* by Julia Cameron

Most Tarcher/Penguin books are available at special quantity discounts for bulk purchase
for sales promotions, premiums, fund-raising, and educational needs. Special books or
book excerpts also can be created to fit specific needs. For details, write Penguin Group
(USA) Inc. Special Markets, 375 Hudson Street,
New York, NY 10014.

Library of Congress Cataloging-in-Publication Data

Cameron, Julia.
The artist's way every day : a year of creative living / Julia Cameron.
p.   cm.
ISBN 978-1-58542-747-5
1. Creation (Literary, artistic, etc.)   2. Self-actualization (Psychology)   I. Cameron,
Julia. Artist's way.   II. Title.
BF408.C1753   2009
701'.15—dc22   2009028958

Printed in the United States of America
1   3   5   7   9   10   8   6   4   2

BOOK DESIGN BY AMANDA DEWEY

Contents

The

ARTIST'S WAY
EVERY DAY

Introduction

On January 25, 1978, I got sober. "Mark this day on your calendar," I was advised. "It's the most important day of your life." I greeted this advice with skepticism. How could a sobriety date be more important than a birthday or a wedding anniversary? It just did not seem possible. Now, thirty-one years later, I recognize the wisdom in singling out that date. I have gone on from there, one day at a time, to maintain my sobriety through both joy and tumult.

"God will never give you more than you can handle," I was told, with the added footnote, "one day at a time." Again, this advice proved wise. On days when my emotional plate felt overladen, I learned to remind myself, "Just one day at a time." Fortunately for me, I got sober in Southern California—sometimes referred to as the "Harvard of Recovery."

"If it's a choice between sobriety and creativity, I don't know that I'll choose sobriety," I complained to my sober mentors in my early months of abstinence.

"There is no choice between sobriety and creativity," they told me. "Without sobriety, there will be no creativity."

And so, I learned that the principle of "one day at a time" applied to my creative life. Pre-sobriety, I had written in binges. Post-sobriety, I learned to write daily, without drama. I was a writer, and writers wrote. Simple as that. "God takes care of the quality; you take care of the quantity," I was advised. "Stop trying to make something up, and try, instead, to get something down." Direction was important here. If I was "making something up," I was straining to reach for something that might be beyond my grasp. If I was "getting something down," I was taking dictation from a higher source.

God is the Great Creator, I came to believe, as I strove to forge an artist-to-artist relationship. I came to believe that creativity is God's will for us, and that we can practice creativity like any other spiritual practice—a day at a time.

In 1980, composer Billy May gave me a tiny but powerful prayer book: *Creative Ideas* by Ernest Holmes. Holmes believed that God's will for us is expansive creativity. Working with his prayers, I came to believe the same thing. Rather than regard myself as the self-conscious author of my work, I began to think of myself more as a conduit, a channel through which the Great Creator's creativity could enter the world.

In 1992, I published *The Artist's Way*—a book which hammered out spiritual principles as a path to higher creativity. To my delight, *The Artist's Way* caught fire. More than three million people purchased the book and employed its principles to expand their creativity. *The Artist's Way* worked as a daily spiritual practice. Its central tool, three pages of longhand morning writing called "Morning Pages," became known as an effective catalyst for personal growth. Many people worked *The Artist's Way* repeatedly, circling back through its pages at ever-increasing depth. As for myself, I have written Morning Pages more than two decades now. They are the bedrock of my spiritual practice; a daily discipline that yields prodigious results.

"Your book changed my life," I am frequently

told. I have come to believe that the daily practice of creativity yields an expanded and deepened sense of spirituality in the lives of Artist's Way practitioners. And so it is with an eye to increasing both creativity and spirituality that I gathered together the teachings found in this book.

I have written more than thirty books using the tools and the concepts that these pages encompass. It is my belief that heightened productivity will come to all who work with them.

JANUARY

January 1

One of the most important tasks in artistic recovery is learning to call things—and ourselves—by the right names. Most of us have spent years using the wrong names for our behaviors. We have wanted to create and we have been unable to create and we have called that inability *laziness*. That is not merely inaccurate. It is cruel. Accuracy and compassion serve us far better. *Blocked artists are not lazy. They are blocked. Do not call the inability to start laziness. Call it fear.*

January 2

It may be useful for you to think of the Morning Pages as meditation. It may not be the practice of meditation you are accustomed to. You may, in fact, not be accustomed to meditating at all. The pages may not seem spiritual or even meditative—more like negative and materialistic, actually—but they are a valid form of meditation that gives us insight and helps us effect change in our lives.

January 3

Looking at God's creation, it is pretty clear that the creator itself did not know when to stop. There is not one pink flower, or even fifty pink flowers, but hundreds. Snowflakes, of course, are the ultimate exercise in sheer creative glee. No two alike. This creator looks suspiciously like someone who just might send us support for our creative ventures.

January 4

Growth is an erratic forward movement: two steps forward, one step back. Remember that and be very gentle with yourself. A creative recovery is a healing process. You may slide backward. This is normal. Growth occurs in spurts. You will lie dormant sometimes. Do not be discouraged. Think of it as resting. Very often, a week of insights will be followed by a week of sluggishness. The Morning Pages will seem pointless. *They are not.* What you are learning to do, writing them even when you are tired and they seem dull, is to rest on the page. This is very important. Marathon runners suggest you log ten slow miles for every fast one. The same holds true for creativity.

January 5

The other basic tool of *The Artist's Way* may strike you as a nontool, a diversion. You may see clearly how Morning Pages could work yet find yourself highly dubious about something called an *Artist Date*. I assure you, Artist Dates work, too. An Artist Date is a block of time, perhaps two hours weekly, especially set aside and committed to nurturing your creative consciousness, your inner artist. In its short primary form, the Artist Date is an excursion, a play date that you preplan and defend against all interlopers. You do not take anyone on this Artist Date but you and your inner artist, a.k.a. your creative child. If you think this sounds stupid or that you will never be able to afford the time, identify that reaction as resistance. You cannot afford not to find time for Artist Dates.

January 6

Many blocked creatives tell themselves they are both too old and too young to allow themselves to pursue their dreams. Old and dotty, they might try it. Young and foolish, they might try it. In either scenario, being crazy is a prerequisite to creative exploration. We do not want to look crazy. And trying something like that (whatever it is) at our age (whatever it is) would look nuts. Yes, maybe. *Creativity occurs in the moment, and in the moment we are timeless.* We discover that as we engage in a creative recovery. "I felt like a kid," we may say after a satisfying Artist Date. Kids are not self-conscious, and once we are actually in the flow of our creativity, neither are we.

January 7

I learned to turn my creativity over to the only god I could believe in, the god of creativity. I learned to get out of the way and let that creative force work through me. I learned to just show up at the page and write down what I heard. I didn't have to be in the mood. I didn't have to take my emotional temperature. I simply wrote. No negotiations. Good, bad? None of my business. I wasn't doing it. By resigning as the self-conscious author, I wrote freely.

January 8

It is never too late to start over. It is never past the point of no return for our artist to recover. We can heap years, decades, a lifetime of insult upon our artist and it is so resilient, so powerful, and so stubborn that it will come back to life when we give it the smallest opportunity. We can help ourselves by coaxing our artist out with the promise of some protected time to be listened to, talked with, and interacted with. If we actively love our artist, our artist will love us in return. Lovers tell secrets and share dreams. Lovers meet no matter how adverse the circumstances, sneaking off for a rendezvous. As we woo our artist with our focused attention and private time, it will reward us with art.

January 9

I have many friends who are not writers, and writing helps them too. As a sort of creative nurse-practitioner, I have sometimes suggested to despairing friends that they give themselves the gift of three longhand pages every morning to see if it doesn't cheer them up. It cheers them up. It energizes them. It gives them a sense of flow.

January 10

One of the chief barriers to accepting God's generosity is our limited notion of what we are in fact able to accomplish. We may tune in to the voice of the creator within, hear a message—and then discount it as crazy or impossible. On the one hand, we take ourselves very seriously and don't want to look like idiots pursuing some patently grandiose scheme. On the other hand, we don't take ourselves—or God—seriously enough and so we define as grandiose many schemes that, with God's help, may fall well within our grasp. Most of us never consider how powerful the creator really is. Instead, we draw very limited amounts of the power available to us. We unconsciously set a limit on how much God can give us or help us. We are stingy with ourselves. And if we receive a gift beyond our imagination, we often send it back. Remembering that God is our source places us in the spiritual position of having an unlimited bank account.

January 11

An artist must have downtime, time to do nothing. Defending our right to such time takes courage, conviction, and resiliency. Such time, space, and quiet will strike our family and friends as a withdrawal from them. It is. For an artist, withdrawal is necessary. Without it, the artist in us feels vexed, angry, out of sorts. If such deprivation continues, our artist becomes sullen, depressed, hostile. We expect our artist to be able to function without giving it what it needs to do so. An artist requires the upkeep of creative solitude. An artist requires the healing of time alone.

January 12

The Morning Pages are the primary tool of creative recovery. Although occasionally colorful, the Morning Pages are often negative, frequently fragmented, often self-pitying, repetitive, stilted or babyish, angry or bland—even silly sounding. Good! All that angry, whiny, petty stuff stands between you and your creativity. Worrying about the job, the laundry, the funny knock in the car, the weird look in your lover's eye—this stuff eddies through our subconscious and muddies our days. Get it on the page.

January 13

In our current culture, writing is discouraged. Hallmark does it for us. We shop for the card that is "closest" to what we wish to say. Schools drill us about how to say what we want to and the how-to involves things like proper spelling, topic sentences, and the avoidance of detours so that logic becomes the field marshal and emotion is kept at bay. Writing, as we are taught to do it, becomes an antihuman activity. We are trained to self-doubt, to self-scrutiny in the place of self-expression. As a result, most of us try to write too carefully. We try to do it "right." We try to sound smart. We try, period. Writing goes much better when we don't work at it so much, when we give ourselves permission to just hang out on the page.

January 14

Life is what we make of it. Whether we conceive of an inner god force or an other, outer God, doesn't matter. Relying on that force does.

January 15

In a sense, our creativity is none of our business. It is a given, not something to be aspired to. It is not an invention of our ego. It is, instead, a natural function of our soul. We are intended to breathe and to live. We are intended to listen and create. We do not need special pens. We do not need special rooms or even special times. What we do need is the intention to allow creativity to create through us. When we open ourselves to something or someone greater than ourselves working through us, we paradoxically open ourselves to our own greatest selves.

January 16

Think of your talent as a young and skittish horse that you are bringing along. This horse is very talented but it is also young, nervous, and inexperienced. It will make mistakes, be frightened by obstacles it hasn't seen before. It may even bolt, try to throw you off, feign lameness. Your job, as the creative jockey, is to keep your horse moving forward and to coax it into finishing the course.

January 17

If you are creatively blocked, it is possible, even probable, that you can learn to create more freely through your willing use of simple tools. Just as doing Hatha Yoga stretches alters consciousness when all you are doing is stretching, doing the exercises in this book alters consciousness when "all" you are doing is writing and playing. Do these things and a break-through will follow—whether you believe in it or not. Whether you call *it* a spiritual awakening or not.

January 18

No matter how secular it may appear, writing is actually a spiritual tool. We undertake it solo, and, not to be too facile with puns, it is worth nothing that that word does have the world "soul" embedded in it. Moving alone onto the page, we often find ourselves companioned by higher forces, by a stream of insights and inspirations that seem somehow "other" than our routine thinking.

January 19

Morning Pages are meditation, a practice that brings you to your creativity and your creator God. In order to stay easily and happily creative, we need to stay spiritually centered. This is easier to do if we allow ourselves centering rituals. It is important that we devise these ourselves from the elements that feel holy and happy to us. A spiritual room or even a spiritual corner is an excellent way to do this. An artist's altar could prove a sensory experience. Burning incense while reading affirmations or writing them, lighting a candle, dancing to drum music, holding a smooth rock or listening to Gregorian chant—all of these tactile, physical techniques reinforce spiritual growth. We need to unlearn our old notion that spirituality and sensuality don't mix. We are meant to celebrate the good things of this earth.

January 20

Artist Dates fire the imagination. They spark whimsy. They encourage play. Since art is about "the play of ideas," Artist Dates feed our work. They gently replenish the inner well. Artist Dates restock our supply of images.

January 21

We all have time to write. We have time to write the minute we are willing to write badly, to chase a dead end, to scribble a few words, to write for the hell of it instead of for the perfect and polished result. The obsession with time is really an obsession with perfection. We want enough time to write perfectly. We want to write with a net under ourselves, a net that says we are not foolish spending our time doing something that might not pay off. When we write from love, when we let ourselves steal minutes as gifts to ourselves, our lives become sweeter, our temperaments become sweeter.

January 22

Creativity is God energy flowing through us, shaped by us, like light flowing through a crystal prism. When we are clear about who we are and what we are doing, the energy flows freely and we experience no strain. When we resist what that energy might show us or where it might take us, we often experience a shaky, out-of-control feeling. We want to shut down the flow and regain our sense of control. We slam on the psychic brakes. Every creative person has myriad ways to block creativity. The choice to block always works in the short run and fails in the long run.

January 23

It is an often repeated spiritual axiom that "when the student is ready, the teacher appears." Over the years, I have heard many stories of miraculous intersections and meetings. The divine mind knows no distance. When we ask to be led, we are led. When we ask to be guided, we are guided. When we ask to be taught, we are taught. Guidance and generosity are always closer at hand than we may think. It always falls to us to be open to receiving guidance and to pray for the willingness and openness to know it when it arrives.

January 24

Art is not about thinking something up. It is about the opposite—getting something down. The directions are important here. If we are trying to *think something up,* we are straining to reach for something that's just beyond our grasp, "up there, in the stratosphere, where art lives on high . . ." When we *get something down,* there is no strain. We're not doing; we're getting. Someone or something else is doing the doing. Instead of reaching for inventions, we are engaged in listening. Art is an act of tuning in and dropping down the well. It is as though all the stories, painting, music, and performances in the world live just under the surface of our normal consciousness. Like an underground river, they flow through us as a stream of ideas that we can tap down into. As artists, we drop down the well into the stream. We hear what's down there and we act on it—more like taking dictation than anything fancy having to do with art.

January 25

The idea that the biggest secret of making art might just be making some art is a conclusion the ego works very hard to avoid. The ego wants us to be "in the mood" to make art at the very least. And yet, as any working artist will honestly tell you, waiting for the mood is a huge time waster. We are married to our art and just as the first caress can lead to interest between a long-married couple, the first lick of work can lead to an appetite for work. In other words, mood more often follows action than instigates.

January 26

"Art" is a form of the verb "to be." It is not mere clev-
erness to point this out. At its core, life is artful and
creative, each moment contains choice as much as each
brush stroke in a painting, each syllable in a poem, each
note in a melodic line. It is because of this, its insistence
on choice, choice, choice, that art demolishes the victim
position. When bullying life demands of us some injus-
tice: "You want to make something of it?" the artful
answer is yes.

January 27

Pivotal to self-expression is the idea that there is a benevolent, interested Universe that wants us to expand. Without such belief, we may buy into our self-doubt and by doing so sharply limit what we are able to attain. We may think, "Wouldn't it be lovely"—but perhaps it could. We must keep focused on the "Perhaps it could."

January 28

Creativity requires faith. Faith requires that we relinquish control. This is frightening, and we resist it. Our resistance to our creativity is a form of self-destruction. We throw up road-blocks on our own path. Why do we do this? In order to maintain an illusion of control. Depression, like anger and anxiety, is resistance, and it creates dis-ease. This manifests itself as sluggishness, confusion, "I don't know . . ." The truth is, we do know and we *know* that we know. Each of us has an inner dream that we can unfold if we will just have the courage to admit what it is. And the faith to trust our own admission. A clearing affirmation can often open the channel. One excellent one is "I know the things I know." Another is "I trust my own inner guide." Either of these will eventually yield us a sense of our own direction. There is a path for each of us. When we are on our right path, we have a sure-footedness. We know the next right action—although not necessarily what is just around the bend. By trusting, we *learn* to trust.

January 29

Anything worth doing is worth doing badly. How we hate *that* idea. We know it as beginners but forget it as we advance. Trial-and-error becomes beneath our dignity. Of course it does. It pulls the rug out from underneath our seriousness. We don't really have a nice big block to stand behind while we "figure things out." What's to figure out? God was humble enough to just doodle, to just noodle, to fool around—why are we so serious?

January 30

When we are using writing to do the work of integration, writing is not only the river but often the bridge across the river. Writing is not only the chasm where we enter in terror to deal with frightening feelings but also the rope we throw across the chasm, the rope we use to pull ourselves to safety. The dailiness of writing allows us not only to walk into change and through it but also to record change in tiny, manageable increments, to find grounding when our lives feel unhorsed.

January 31

Remember that art is process. The process is supposed to be fun. For our purposes, "the journey is always the only arrival" may be interpreted to mean that our creative work is actually our creativity itself at play in the field of time. At the heart of this play is the mystery of joy.

FEBRUARY

February 1

You say you want to make art. You want to begin or you want to continue. This is good. We need a more artful world, and that means we need you and the specific contribution that you and you alone can make. But to make it you must start somewhere, and that is often the sticking point. We all have our fears, and they feel as real as the chair you are sitting in. Like that chair, they can be slouched into or left behind. Sometimes we need to sit up and ignore the cricks in our back and shoulders and just begin. That's how it is with art. We just need to begin. Begin where you are, with *who* you are. In order to go where you want to go creatively, you have to start somewhere. And the best place to start is precisely where you are. This is true whether you are a beginning artist or someone with long miles down the track. In fact, seasoned artists can waste time and energy mulling the dignity of their acquired position in the field when the truth is, they still need to just start again.

February 2

I believe and know creativity to be a spiritual issue. "Faith moves mountains"—Christ told us that, and he may have meant that literally. We speak of the Great Creator, we speak of Christ but seldom make the connection that the spiritual laws he taught are actually the spiritual laws related to creativity. "Knock and it shall be opened." "Ask and you shall receive"—these are spiritual laws as they relate to manifestation. As artists, we routinely ask for inspiration. We need to learn from Christ's example that we can also ask for the material manifestation of our visions to come to us as money, support, opportunity. Our faith, which is a request coupled with an expectation of its successful fulfillment, is no different from the faith of a navigator setting out to prove the world is round. Creative dreams come to us as visions that we are charged with fulfilling. When we allow the Great Creator to do this to us, through us, then we are aligning ourselves with the spiritual power necessary to negate the "odds."

February 3

QUESTION: What would I do if I didn't have to do it perfectly?

ANSWER: A great deal more than I am.

We've all heard that the unexamined life is not worth living, but consider too that the unlived life is not worth examining. The success of a creative recovery hinges on our ability to move out of the head and into action. This brings us squarely to risk. Most of us are practiced at talking ourselves out of risk. We are skilled speculators on the probably pain of self-exposure. We deny that in order to do something well we must first be willing to do it badly. Once we are willing to accept that anything worth doing might even be worth doing badly our options widen.

February 4

Optimism is critical to our spiritual health. Is our creative glass half full or half empty? It's a matter of perception—and faith. For most of us, the idea that we can listen to ourselves, trust ourselves, and value ourselves is a radical leap of faith. The idea that we can tell ourselves "Hey, you are doing pretty well and so much better than you did last year" amounts to a revolution. The possibility that we can trust ourselves, our decisions, and our painstaking progress, that this trust might be enough, even admirable, requires that we muster a soupçon of optimism. Optimism about ourselves and our chances is an elected attitude. We can choose to believe the best and not the worst, but to do that we must become conscious of our own negative voice-over and decide to change our mental sound track.

February 5

For artists, optimism is a great advantage. It is too easy to buy into pessimism, to romance the many odds so clearly stacked against us. It is easy to give in and to give up. But is it really so easy to let dreams die? Dreams are hardy. They are stubborn as weeds. We may think we have uprooted our dreams only to have a dream push upward again, daring us, one more time, to believe in the unbelievable. As long as a dream lives, so does a chance of its manifesting. We can cooperate with our dreams or we can fight them. Our dreams are tenacious. They don't just fade away.

February 6

Creativity is a spiritual practice. It is not something that can be perfected, finished, and set aside. It is my experience that we reach plateaus of creative attainment only to have a certain restlessness set in. Yes, we are successful. Yes, we have made it but . . . This unfinished quality, this restless appetite for further exploration, tests us. We are asked to expand in order that we not contract. As artists, we are spiritual sharks. The ruthless truth is that if we don't keep moving, we sink to the bottom and die. The choice is very simple: we can insist on resting on our laurels, or we can begin anew. The stringent requirement of a sustained creative life is the humility to start again, to begin anew.

February 7

Out of the notion, "I can" comes the next thought: "I think I will." The impulse is playful. It doesn't consider the odds. It is an impulse born of pure faith. The artist has a vision and that vision includes the successful completion of the art he has in mind. An artist is like a lover who cannot pause to entertain the possibility of being spurned. He must press his suit. His whole impulse is to love.

February 8

It is my belief that writing is a way to bless and to multiply our blessings. I cherish letters, postcards, faxes, notes, and even Post-its from my friends. We are so skilled in the art of negative imagination, we are adroit at the art of writing out of anxiety, what might our writing and our world look like if we allowed ourselves to inhabit our positive imagination?

February 9

Writing is about honesty. It is almost impossible to be honest and boring at the same time. Being honest may be many other things—risky, scary, difficult, frightening, embarrassing, and hard to do—but it is not boring. Whenever I am stuck in a piece of writing, I ask myself, "Am I failing to tell the truth? Is there something I am not saying, something I am afraid to say?" Telling the truth on the page, like telling the truth in a relationship, always takes you deeper.

February 10

All of us are creative. Some of us get the mirroring to know we are creative, but few of us get the mirroring to know *how* creative. What most of us get is the worried advice that if we are thinking about a life in the arts, we'd better plan to have "something to fall back on." Would they tell us that if we expressed an interest in banking? It could be argued that as people and as artists, we are what we are—however, we also become ourselves, *all* of ourselves, by having our largeness mirrored back to us. Too often we lack such mirrors. No magic wand taps our life to make us into what we dream.

February 11

Opening to our intuition is like opening to a new love affair. Our first adventure may be a coffee date that feels a little stiff but has a few memorable possibilities. Our second flyer may be a little more bold—say, a kiss good-bye on the cheek. Our third venture may mark the beginning of a budding passion, an interest that we can't quite shake, that companions us through our days. An intuitive leading is a lead we must follow. "Destiny" arrives as a humble lunch, not a fanfare.

February 12

The process of identifying a *self* inevitably involves loss as well as gain. We discover our boundaries, and those boundaries by definition separate us from our fellows. As we clarify our perceptions, we lose our misconceptions. As we eliminate ambiguity, we lose illusion as well. We arrive at clarity, and clarity creates change.

February 13

Just as walking aerobicizes the physical body, producing a flow of endorphins and good feelings, writing seems to alter the chemical balance of the soul itself, restoring balance and equilibrium when we are out of sorts, bringing clarity, a sense of right action, a feeling of purpose to a rudderless day. Furthermore, writing when we are out of happiness can lead us into writing from happiness. We recall happier moments and we recall happiness itself.

February 14

As artists, we often speak of our creations as our "brainchildren," but we forget that our ideas and dreams impregnate us. We are inhabited by a larger life than we know. As we doubt our own identity, that identity is still guiding us, still nudging us to our rightful path. We may doubt our creative viability but, like children who *will* be born, our dreams and desires nudge us forward. Something larger and finer than we know calls us to be larger and finer than we dare. So we act on faith, descend into doubt, and watch in amazement as our dreams carry us forward with a knowing of their own. Sometimes our dreams feel born despite us.

February 15

G o to an office supply or art supply shop. Acquire a small blank notebook suitable for sketching. Carry this notebook with you and carry, too, a sketching pencil or pen so that you can begin to capture the many small adventures of life as you actually live it. So much of the adventure of the life we lead rushes past us in a blur. Velocity is the culprit. Velocity and pressure. A sketch-book freezes time. It is an instantaneous form of meditation focusing us on the worth of every passing moment. So often the great adventure of life lies between the lines, in how we felt at a certain time and at a certain place. This tool will help you to remember and savor the passing parade.

February 16

So much has been written about the loneliness of the writer's lot that if feels like heresy to report the truth as I know it: in my experience, *not* writing is a lonely business. The minute I let myself write, everything else falls into balance. If I get a dose of writing in my day, then I can actually socialize with a clear conscience. I can actually be present for the life I am having rather than living in the never-never land of the nonwriting writer, that twilight place where you always "should" be somewhere else—writing—so that you can never enjoy where you actually are.

February 17

People frequently believe the creative life is grounded in fantasy. The more difficult truth is that creativity is grounded in reality, in the particular, the focused, the well observed or specifically imagined. As we lose our vagueness about our self, our values, our life situation, we become available to the moment. It is there, in the particular, that we contact the creative self. Until we experience the freedom of solitude, we cannot connect authentically. We may be enmeshed, but we are not encountered. Art lies in the moment of encounter: we meet our truth and we meet ourselves; we meet ourselves and we meet our self-expression. We become original because we become something specific: an origin from which work flows.

February 18

Art is an image-using system. In order to create, we draw from our inner well. This inner well, an artistic reservoir, is ideally like a well-stocked trout pond. We've got big fish, little fish, fat fish, skinny fish—an abundance of artistic fish to fry. As artists, we must realize that we have to maintain this artistic ecosystem. If we don't give some attention to upkeep, our well is apt to become depleted, stagnant, or blocked. Any extended period or piece of work draws heavily on our artistic well. As artists, we must learn to be self-nourishing. We must become alert enough to consciously replenish our creative resources as we draw on them—to restock the trout pond, so to speak. I call this process *filling the well*.

February 19

To be an artist of depth, one cultivates a level of sensitivity that is acute. Performing artists, for example, listen with an ear cocked to the spiritual questions posed by a great piece of music or a great part onstage, and they open themselves to receive the energies required to manifest those questions creatively. Tackling those towering creative pinnacles, they are like tender birds who have learned to perch on skyscrapers as well as on trees. They still have all the acute sensitivity they have ever had, and they have also adapted enough to live in the fiercely competitive winds of high-altitude performance—but this does not mean it is easy. Artists facing an Olympian role *are* like athletes—highly trained, highly strung, and highly susceptible to injury, physical and psychic.

February 20

Art is alchemy. It turns the ore of life into gold. Learning to make art rather than drama from a heated imagination is a skill best learned early and practiced fully. If we are to make living art—*and* an art of living—we must be willing to stand knee-deep in the rapids of the human condition, accepting that life, by its nature, is turbulent, powerful, and mysterious. It is the artist's bet that life is better encountered and expressed than diminished and discounted by trying to "fix it" therapeutically. It is the artist's conviction that understanding something intellectually is often far less healing than making something artistically transformative from our shattered selves.

February 21

Most blocked creatives are cerebral beings. We think of all the things we want to do but can't. In order to effect a real recovery, one that lasts, we need to move out of the head and into a body of work. To do this, we must first of all move *into the body*. What we are after here is a *moving* meditation. This means one where the act of motion puts us into the now and helps us to stop spinning. Twenty minutes a day is sufficient. The object is to stretch your mind more than your body, so there doesn't need to be an emphasis on fitness, although eventual fitness is a likely result. The goal is to connect to a world outside of us, to lose the obsessive self-focus of self-exploration and, simply, explore. One quickly notes that when the mind is focused on *other,* the self often comes into a far more accurate focus.

February 22

Nelson Mandela has remarked that we do no one any favors "hiding our light" and pretending to be "smaller than we are." And yet, calling it modesty, we often try and play small and even stay small. When the creative power moving through us asks us to expand, we would rather contract, calling it more comfortable—it isn't really. We are spiritual beings, and when our spirit grows larger, so must we. There will be no comfortable resting in yesterday's definition of ourselves. It is spiritual law that as the Great Creator is always exploring, experiencing, and expanding through its creations, we must cooperate or feel the pinch of spiritual dis-ease. We can try to play small, but if the universe has big plans for us, we are better off cooperating than resisting. Creativity is God's true nature and our own. As we surrender to becoming as large as we are meant to be, great events can come to pass for us and countless others. In a sense, the size the Great Creator makes of us is none of our business. We work on art and we are the Great Creator's work of art. Perhaps we shouldn't meddle.

February 23

Writing is the act of motion. Writing is the commitment to move forward, not to stew in our own juices, to become whatever it is that we are becoming. Writing is both the boat and the wind in the sails. Even on the days when the winds of inspiration seem slight, there is some forward motion, some progress made.

February 24

One of our chief needs as creative beings is support. Unfortunately, this can be hard to come by. Ideally, we would be nurtured and encouraged first by our nuclear family and then by ever-widening circles of friends, teachers, well-wishers. As young artists, we need to want to be acknowledged for our attempts and efforts as well as for our achievements and triumphs. Unfortunately, many artists never receive this critical early encouragement. As a result, they may not know they are artists at all.

February 25

Since our mythology would have us believe that artists are by nature wild and careless, why worry about our fiscal health? Because we are all inwardly wealthy and we can squander our inner wealth the way a fool squanders a fortune. How do we squander our wealth? To begin with, we show our work too soon and too indiscriminately. We undervalue our valuable writing. We do not qualify our readers the way a bank qualifies an investor. We do not stop to question the aspiring reader's qualifications. In our eagerness to be read, we open the city gates. This is like giving passersby access to our checking account.

February 26

As artists we must learn who and what to give a wide berth. We must steer clear, if we can, of people who dampen our enthusiasms, who cut short our flights of fancy. Like the sharp-taloned owl, a sharp tongue goaded by cynicism can quickly tear our optimism to shreds. We are resilient but delicate. We must be alert. We must be vigilant. We cannot control everyone around us, but we can learn whose company is good for us and whose company causes us to shrivel and shrink.

February 27

Mystery is at the heart of creativity. That, and surprise. All too often, when we say we want to be creative, we mean that we want to be able to be productive. Now, to be creative *is* to be productive—but by cooperating with the creative process, not forcing it. As creative channels, we need to trust the darkness. We need to learn to gently mull instead of churning away on a straight-ahead path. Hatching an idea is a lot like baking bread. An idea needs to rise. If you poke at it too much at the beginning, if you keep checking on it, it will never rise. A loaf of bread must stay for a good long time in the darkness and safety of the oven. Open that oven too soon and the bread collapses. Creativity requires a respectful reticence. The truth is that this is how to raise the best ideas. Let them grow in dark and mystery. Let them form on the roof of our consciousness. Let them hit the page in droplets. Trusting this slow and seemingly random drip, we will be startled one day by the flash of "Oh! That's *it!*"

February 28

We must write from love and we must choose those to read us who read from love: the love of words. The love of naming our experience must finally be the guiding force in what we put on the page. When we write from fear of criticism, we hamper our stride and we cripple our voice. When we choose as readers those who love to criticize rather than those who love to read, we invite catastrophe.

February 29

It takes courage to put ourselves out on the page, but it is better to be in reality than in denial. Reality is a place to start something. Denial is a place where something is already going on that we do not want to see and be a part of even though we are. When most of us say we are zeroed out, we are in fact someplace we can start from, not nowhere at all. The trick, the first trick, lies in admitting exactly where we are.

MARCH

March 1

In order to grow as artists, we must be willing to risk. We must try to do something more and larger than what we have done before. We cannot continue indefinitely to replicate the successes of our past. Great careers are characterized by great risks. It takes courage to jettison the mantle of what we have done well for the chance to grab at the cape of what we might do even better. We cannot play it safe and expand as artists at the same time. We must risk expanding our territory. There are certain risks that come with pursuing an artistic career. Our reward must lie in the risk itself, in the self-esteem we feel for undertaking it.

March 2

It is difficult to overemphasize the amount of care that must be taken to protect our writing. While we cannot control or in any way guarantee our writing's reception in the public sphere, we can control and to a degree guarantee the reception of our writing in the private sphere. Do not be self-destructive in your choice of early readers.

March 3

In order to thrive as artists—and, one could argue, as people—we need to be available to the universal flow. When we put a stopper on our capacity for joy by anorectically declining the small gifts of life, we turn aside the larger gifts as well. Those of us who have stymied the work flow completely will find ourselves in lives that feel barren and devoid of interest no matter how many meaningless things we have filled them with. What gives us true joy? That is the question to ask.

March 4

Daily writing, writing simply for the sake of writing, is like keeping a pot of soup on the back of the stove: it is always there, always ready to be tasted, always ready to be added to, always nourishing, savory, life-sustaining. Like soup, your daily writing doesn't have to be fancy. A few simple ingredients are enough. Honesty, observation, and imagination are the three ingredients that are the staples. They make up the broth, the basic stock that the rest comes from and adds to.

March 5

Doubt is a signal of the creative process. It is a signal that you are doing something right—not that you are doing something wrong or crazy or stupid. The sickening chasm of fear that doubt triggers to yawn open beneath you is not a huge abyss into which you are going to tumble, spiraling downward like you are falling through the circles of hell. No, doubt is most often a signal you are doing something and doing it right.

March 6

Creativity is a lamp, not a candle. Something wants to write through us as badly as we want to write. Discovering this is a matter of time and patience.

March 7

The truth that we are intended to express is that we are all larger than we know. We are part of a grand design. There is room for our expansion. The Universe falls in with worthy plans. As we strive to grow larger and more expansive, the Universe seeks to expand through us. When we reach for support, the support is there. Our expansion is planned for, even counted upon. If we do not expand, the Universe cannot expand. If we thwart our true nature, we also thwart God's.

March 8

It takes an effort to be clear about things. It is easier and much sadder to be muddy, to never take the time to clarify our thoughts and connect to our own perceptions. The act of paying attention is what brings us peace. In meditation we pay attention to the breath or to the image or to the mantra. We concentrate on something, and that concentration, that stillness, brings us to the point of knowing that we are all right, that God is in his heaven and all is right with the world—even if we believe in no God and no heaven. The act of concentration is that powerful, that filled with blessings.

March 9

Art is not linear. Neither is the artist's life, but we forget that. We try to "plan" our life and "plan" our career—as if we could. We also try to plan our growth. This means transformation catches us by surprise. The notion that we can control our path is pushed on us by advertisements and by books and by experts who promise us we can learn to control the uncontrollable. And yet, experience teaches that life, and especially life in the arts, is as much about mystery as it is about mastery. To be successful we must learn to follow not the leader but our own inner leadings, the "inspiration" artists have acknowledged through the centuries. "Something" is telling us to make art. We must trust that something.

March 10

Although we seldom talk about it in these terms, writing is a means of prayer. It connects us to the invisible world. It gives us a gate for the other world to talk to us whether we call it the subconscious, the unconscious, the superconscious, the imagination, or the Muse. Writing gives us a place to welcome more than the rational. It opens the door to inspiration. Writing is a spiritual housekeeper. Writing sets things straight, giving us a sense of our true priorities.

March 11

"Where does this thought go?" We start to chase our consciousness a little. We are roused out of our torpor, our ennui. Life becomes a matter of some interest and we become the interested bystanders and then the participants. All of this happens because we connect. All of this happens a page at a time, a pen stroke at a time. SCRATCH. Start from scratch. Just move your pen across the page and watch what happens to you.

March 12

For most of us, the idea that the creator encourages creativity is a radical thought. We tend to think, or at least fear, that creative dreams are egotistical, something that God wouldn't approve of for us. After all, our creative artist is an inner youngster and prone to childish thinking. If our mom or dad expressed doubt or disapproval for our creative dreams, we may project that same attitude onto a parental god. This thinking must be undone.

March 13

There is an uncanny Something that kicks in as the result of prayer. I may find myself at my desk, writing for longer hours than is my usual wont. I may find myself writing with greater candor, risking a self-revelation that I might normally have eschewed. When an artist is fully engaged in working, there is a self-forgetting that happens. The artist becomes absorbed in the service of work that he is creating. The ego dissolves and the soul steps forward.

March 14

When we move toward our own creativity, we move toward our Creator. When we seek to become more spiritual, we find ourselves becoming more creative. Our creativity and our spirituality are so closely interconnected they are in effect one and the same thing. Speaking of God, we often use the terms "Maker" or "Creator" without recognizing that those are the terms for "artist." God is the Great Artist. We are creations and we are intended, in turn, to be creative ourselves.

March 15

As artists, we must learn to try. We must learn to act affirmatively. We must learn to act as though spring is at hand—because it is. We are the spring that we are waiting for. Wherever creativity is afoot, so is a blossoming. All creative acts are acts of initiative. In order to make art, we must be willing to labor. We must be willing to reach inside and draw forth what we find there. On an inner plane, we are all connected to a larger whole. This is what is meant by inspiration, this connection to something greater than ourselves. But it begins with where we are and what we are. It begins with possibility.

March 16

Part of husbanding our talent lies in finding those who are generous enough to reflect us back as talented. Creativity flourishes in an atmosphere of acceptance. As we learn to number friends to our work among our friends, that work can strengthen and bloom. Believing mirrors are believers, first of all, in the basic good of life. Setting aside chic skepticism, they are upbeat and encouraging. They believe in the college try. What's more, they believe in trying again. They are realists. They expect good things, but they know good things take work. They assume you will do the work because your dreams are good and worthy. They will help you if they can. It could be argued that friendship is often the determining factor between a career that flourishes and one that languishes. We are responsible for choosing our friends.

March 17

What if writing were approached like white-water rafting? Something to try just for the fact of having tried it, for the spills and chills of having gone through the rapids of the creative process. What if we allowed ourselves to be amateurs (from the Latin verb *amare,* "to love"). If we could just get over the auditioning to be respected at this aspect, a great many people might love writing. Although our mythology seldom tells us this, it's fun.

March 18

Art is the act of structuring time. "Look at it this way," a piece of art says. "Here's how I see it." This is particularly true when what we are dealing with is an artistic loss. Every loss must always be viewed as a potential gain. Every end is a beginning. We know that. But we tend to forget it as we move through grief. Struck by a loss, we focus, understandably, on what we leave behind. We need to focus on what lies ahead. This can be tricky. We may not know what lies ahead. And, if the present hurts this badly, we tend to view the future as impending pain. "Gain disguised as loss" is a potent artist's tool. To acquire it, simply, brutally, ask: "How can this loss serve me? Where does it point my work?" The answers will surprise and liberate you. The trick is to metabolize pain as energy. The key to doing that is to know, to trust, and to act as if a silver lining exists if you are only willing to look at the work differently or walk through a different door.

March 19

Gentleness, encouragement, safety—these are the watchwords to be put in place for criticism. I have been writing for thirty years. I have seen more good writing destroyed by bad criticism than I have ever seen bad writing helped by good criticism. I have watched valid and valuable books be picked to pieces by too many editors. I have watched plays start to find their feet, only to be tripped up by too many people contributing fixes. It is a metaphysical law that "the first rule of magic is containment." Nowhere should that law be more rigorously applied than to our writing.

March 20

Your artist is a child. Spending time in solitude with your artist child is essential to self-nurturing. A long country walk, a solitary expedition to the beach for a sunrise or sunset, a sortie out to a strange church to hear gospel music, to an ethnic neighborhood to taste foreign sights and sounds—your artist might enjoy any of these. Or your artist might like bowling.

March 21

Our creations are like children. They can be pushy about what they want and what they need. If we neglect them, they neglect us. If we ignore them, they ignore us. Sometimes they sulk and pout and cry and squabble until they've got our attention. In the end, we have to do what they want. It's the only way to make peace with them. Making peace with our creations is an artist's primary task.

March 22

When someone who ignites our creative imagination crosses our path, that person is a "fuse lighter." Our creative engine kicks over. We suddenly have things to say and long for new ways to say them. We suddenly "come alive to the possibility." We are galvanized. In a sense we are in love—and we are also in love with our own artist, who is suddenly mirrored back to us as exciting and adventurous, powerful, perhaps even dangerous. We experience more energy. We burn the candle at both ends, staying up late to work on a project. Getting up early to grab an hour at the easel, like a stolen bout of lovemaking on the way to work. Creative energy and sexual energy are both personal energy. Our use of them is private, and to pretend otherwise is debilitating and abusive. In point of fact, the two energies are so closely intertwined, they may be experienced as nearly identical. We conceive children and we conceive creative projects. Both energies are sacred.

March 23

Healing is a somewhat automatic by-product of self-expression, not a goal per se. This fact can confuse some people—particularly therapists, who want to "understand" the workings of a process that is both mysterious and spiritual. Intellectually, many doctors and therapists do know that something heals beyond their own skill, but understandably, they want to know what that something is, and control it as part of the healing process that they can administer like a good medicine. Therapy and creative recovery are not mutually exclusive, but they do function differently and come out of two very different sets of assumptions. Humans are complex, creative beings, and when we create something that expresses our own complexity, we arrive at an inner distillate of clarity through our own *creative* inner process.

March 24

Insight in and of itself is an intellectual comfort. Power in and of itself is a blind force that can destroy as easily as build. It is only when we consciously learn to link power and light that we begin to feel our rightful identities as creative beings. The Morning Pages allow us to forge this link. They provide us with a spiritual ham-radio set to contact the Creator Within. For this reason, the Morning Pages are a spiritual practice.

March 25

All human beings are creative. The more we can accept and welcome that fact, the more normal our own creativity can become. If it is "normal," then it can be shared with everyone. If it can be shared with everyone, then there is lots of help available to us when we get discouraged. We don't feel inspired, far from it, but we begin anyway and something in the act of beginning seems to jump-start a flow of ideas. In cozy retrospect, we can call such ideas "inspiration," but as they occur they are far more workaday. One thing seems to lead to another and another, and before we know it an "inspired" day's work has transpired. The only genuinely inspired part of that day was the very beginning when we decided to accept the Nike slogan, "Just do it."

March 26

Until one is committed, there is hesitancy, the chance to draw back, always ineffectiveness. Concerning all acts of initiative (or creation) there is one elementary truth, the ignorance of which kills countless ideas and splendid plans: that the moment one definitely commits oneself, then Providence moves too. All sorts of things occur to help one that would otherwise never have occurred. A whole stream of events issues from the decision, raising in one's favor all manner of incidents and meetings and material assistance which no man would have believed would have come his way.

March 27

When we think about publishing, we think in terms of lucky breaks. We do not think in terms of making our own luck, manufacturing our own breaks. And yet, a startling percentage of the books that make it to our best-seller lists began as someone's stubborn idea, stubbornly self-published. And, quite apart from best-seller lists and "beating the odds," there is the solid satisfaction of the modest yet fully realized success of seeing the book in our mind become the book held in our hand.

March 28

In order to succeed as an artist we must have two well-developed functions: our artist and its trainer. The trainer is steady and adult. It keeps its eye on the course and the long run. It coaxes, wheedles, begs, cajoles, and occasionally disciplines our artist which, childlike, proceeds in spurts and sometimes not at all. The trick is setting the jumps low enough that our artist can be lured into action. If I am writing nonfiction, I set my goal at a modest three pages. Almost anyone can write three pages of something and my artist knows that. If we set our jumps low enough, our artist can be lured into cooperation.

March 29

Our bodies are storytellers. We store memories in our bodies. We store passion and heartache. We store joy, moments of transcendent peace. If we are to access these, if we are to move into them and through them, we must enter our bodies to do so. When we encounter an emotional shock, the trauma of a lost beloved, the grief of separation, our bodies count the cost. Our minds may go numb, adroit at denial, but our bodies hold fast to the truth.

March 30

When we become willing to be an empty vessel, we must let go of ideas of how our work should look and should sound. It is the same problem for writers as it is for actors. If an actor has an "idea" of the performance he is trying to give, that concept gets in the way of being true to the moment-to-moment life that is trying to move through him. Similarly, as writers, if we spend too much time conceptualizing our work rather than actualizing it, we become stuck in how something should look and that leaves us caught on a surface level when the work itself may wish to move deeper.

March 31

Recovering from artist's block, like recovering from any major illness or injury, requires a commitment to health. At some point, we must make an active choice to relinquish the joys and privileges accorded to the emotional invalid. A productive artist is quite often a happy person. This can be very threatening as a self-concept to those who are used to getting their needs met by being unhappy. We get more sympathy as crippled artists than as functional ones. Those of us addicted to sympathy in the place of creativity can become increasingly threatened as we become increasingly functional. Many recovering artists become so threatened that they make U-turns and sabotage themselves. In dealing with our creative U-turns, we must first of all extend ourselves some sympathy. A successful creative career is always built on successful creative failures. The trick is to survive them. It helps to remember that even our most illustrious artists have taken creative U-turns in their time.

APRIL

April 1

I t is all too easy to think of art as something we aspire to, an ideal by which to measure our efforts and find them falling woefully short. Well, that is one way to think of art, and God knows we have bludgeoned ourselves with it pretty thoroughly. Our concepts of "great art" and "great artists" are often less something we aspire to than something we use to denigrate our own effort. We might want to try thinking about art a little differently. "Art" is less about what we could be and more about what we are than we normally acknowledge. When we are fixated on getting better, we miss what it is we already are—and this is dangerous because we—as we are—are the origin of our art. "We" are what makes our art original. If we are always striving to be something more and something different, we dilute the power of what it is we actually are. Doing that, we dilute our art.

April 2

It is one of the mysterious happinesses of the creative life that when we become willing to listen, the "still, small voice" seems to grow louder. The web of life is interconnected and an artist's prayer in Omaha is as clearly heard as the same prayer uttered in Manhattan. "Help me become what I am," we pray—and we do. By listening to our heart's desires and listening to them closely, we are not only led into making the art we dream of making but also into the dream of that art being realized on a meaningful scale. Like the farmer in *Field of Dreams,* we must trust enough to build it—whatever "it" is—and trust that "they" will come.

April 3

The human being does not exist who has not procrastinated. Many human beings have devised stratagems to deal with their procrastination. Suddenly, we can avail ourselves of their help. We don't need to talk to another writer to be understood. "I know I should, but I just can't make myself" is something anyone can understand. Suddenly starting on the novel is just a chore, no more glorified than cleaning out the broom closet. You'll feel better once you've made a stab at it. Which you can, with a little help from your friends.

April 4

God is present everywhere. The act of making art is a direct path to contact with God, and we do not need to travel any geographic or psychic distance to experience the grace of creation in the grace of our own creating. Goethe told us, "Whatever you think you can do, or believe you can do, begin it, because action has magic, grace and power in it." This was no mere bromide. It was a report on spiritual experience—an experience that each of us can have whenever we surrender to being a beginner, whenever we dismantle our adult's aloof avoidance and actively seek the Great Creator's hand by reaching out our own to start anew.

April 5

We're fed a great deal of romance surrounding the lonely lot of the artist. Over a recent weekend, teaching in San Francisco, I asked for a show of hands from all the people who believed an artist's life would be lonely. In a room filled with two hundred people, nearly two hundred hands went up. Believing this, we can try to live it out—a prospect that makes for a great deal of pain. The truth is that creativity occurs in clusters. Consider Paris in the twenties and the cluster that built up around Gertrude Stein's hospitality. Consider the Bloomsbury Group convening for Thursday-night cocktails and inadvertently launching a movement. It can be argued that successful art is built on successful friendships. It can certainly be said that friends are what enable an artist to go the distance.

April 6

As artists, we run a risk of staleness if we close ourselves off to fresh experience. Each day must remain an exploratory expedition. We must remain tourists on our home terrain. We must hold on to a sense of adventure. To do this, we must keep our curiosity alive and gently feed it. Walking, the world moves toward us at a manageable rate. We are able to take in the new flowers at the greengrocer's, the fresh plantings in a window box. We see our world anew.

April 7

If we will use writing to connect to ourselves, I believe we can connect across time and space and distance. I believe in the global village we are making, and I believe that in order to make that village truly habitable, we will need to return to the page. We use the expression "I am paging him" when we speak of trying to get someone's attention at some busy intersection—a convention, an international airport, a large manufacturing concern. Our world, our global village, is all of these things, and if we want to get one another's attention, we do need to "page," in the slightly different sense that we need to write.

April 8

Writing is best broken down into a one-day-at-a-time, one-page-at-a-time process. We do not need the courage to write a whole novel. We need the courage only to write on the novel today. We do not need the courage to finish and publish a novel all in one fell swoop. All we need is the courage to do the next right thing. Today's pages may yield tomorrow's editing job and next month's design job, but just for today all we need to do is write.

April 9

If you ask an artist how he got where he is, he will not describe breaking in but instead will talk of a series of lucky breaks. "A thousand unseen helping hands," Joseph Campbell calls these breaks. I call them synchronicity. It is my contention that you can count on them. Take a small step in the direction of a dream and watch the synchronous doors flying open. Seeing, after all, is believing. And if you see the results of your experiments, you will not need to believe me. "Leap, and the net will appear."

April 10

As artists, we have a different kind of accountability than many people. What pays us and pays off in the long run is really the caliber of our work. As artists, we have an inner Geiger counter and it ticks loud and clear when we are near pay dirt—first-rate, high-caliber ore that means we are working at the top of our form. Because this device is an inner one, it isn't easily fooled by the prestige of a certain venue or the lack of another. What it detects is quality. It knows the real thing when it is near it. This is what "accountability" is for an artist, the blunt assessment: Is it any good? It boils down to the simple fact that artists respect good art—and we respect ourselves when we make it.

April 11

Making a piece of art may feel a lot like telling a family secret. Secret telling, by its very nature, involves shame and fear. It asks the question "What will they think of me once they know this?" This is a frightening question, particularly if we have ever been made to feel ashamed for our curiosities and explorations—social, sexual, spiritual. The act of making art exposes a society to itself. Art brings things to light. It illuminates us. It sheds light on our lingering darkness. It casts a beam into the heart of our own darkness and says, "See?"

April 12

If you think of the universe as a vast electrical sea in which you are immersed and from which you are formed, opening to your creativity changes you from something bobbing in that sea to a more fully functioning, more conscious, more cooperative part of that ecosystem.

April 13

We are the Universe. We are made of it and it is made of us. If it is intelligent, we are intelligent. If it is wise and all-knowing, so are we. If it knows what is best for us, we too know what is best. There is no separation between God and us, God and matter. It is all consciousness. We are all consciousness. We are God dreaming God. We are God making God. We are creators co-creating the Universe. If we can trust the Universe, then we can trust ourselves. Even better, if we can trust ourselves, then we can trust the Universe.

April 14

For an artist, "I don't know" is the hard time. It is the season between seasons when you are not sure what you are making and if you are making anything worthwhile. All artists go through seasons of rooted joy and seasons of rootless restlessness and doubt. It goes with the territory. If we knew, always, what it is we know, there would be no new land to push forward to. We would do and redo what it is we do—and that is not the artist's life. Ours is a life of invention.

April 15

Who says (besides our Inner Perfectionist, who is always doing sit-ups) that we have to feel calm and centered to write out a piece of music? Maybe we can feel and be a wreck and do it anyway. Maybe we can do it and do it wrong and fix it later. Maybe we do not have to be or perform perfectly. Maybe we are allowed to have a learning curve. Maybe part of what we need to learn is a little compassion.

April 16

Wanting to know where we are going is often how we fail to go anywhere at all. Rather than surrender to the mystery of the creative journey, we want to know each sight we will see, each obstacle we will confront. Each "something" that we will encounter if we dare to begin. The truth is that we cannot know where our creative trail is taking us. We cannot predict precisely who and what it is we will become. The only certainty is that we will change from who and what we are. We will become something larger and something more, but exactly the form that something more and larger will take is a creation that we have not yet created and cannot demand to know.

April 17

By breaking our life down into daily bites, we all have far more strength than we may realize. It is possible to make the best of a difficult situation "one day at a time." It is a discipline that we must set for ourselves, the narrowing of life's scope to a manageable amount. Just for today, we are able to do the best we can with our child. Just for today, we can get our dog out for an outing. Just for today, we can soldier on. As an artist, soldiering on is often what is called for. We may not be able to see any opening, any sure path for our work to follow. But it is not hopeless. If we are willing to soldier on, there are bright days ahead of us as well as dark. If we muster the courage to continue, there is hope that we might succeed. We need to focus on the possible positive. We need to count on ourselves and on a benevolent larger power that wishes us well.

April 18

As artists, we are ever companioned by the Great Artist. We are being nudged ever so gently forward, urged to continue making what it is that we make. There is no moment at which we are alone, even though our mythology makes much of artists as loners. We are not loners—certainly not spiritually. There is a higher octave that is always available to us. We need only to keep one ear cocked. There it is: the still, small voice. It comes to us in all times at all places. We are never unpartnered, never solitary although we may, to the casual eye, make our art "alone."

April 19

Each of us is unique and irreplaceable. There is only one of us in all of time. We are on this earth, partnered always by unseen forces that would guide us and guard us as we journey into the unknown. No one else can take our journey for us. Two people setting off side by side will still encounter different sights, different wonders. The openness to being is all the openness we are required to have each day. We start today, and tomorrow we start again, and the day after we start again, as we will the day after that. In this way, and no other, does our journey come to us. We begin. The rest unfolds through us.

April 20

It is the ego's dicey proposition that as artists we should always be "special" and different. The ego likes to be set apart. It likes to look down its nose at the rest of humanity. Such isolation is actually damaging. It is like the reverse of the Midas touch turning everything golden into a problem. Let us say we have fear—as all humans do—the ego would have us having "artistic fear" which sounds like a specialized something that perhaps only an expert, and an expensive expert at that, could help us cope with. If we have plain old ordinary fear then we are within reach of a solution. Fear has been with humankind for millennia and we do know what to do about it—pray about it, talk about it, feel the fear, and do it anyway. It is only by courting humility that we stand a chance as artists. When we choose to join the human condition rather than set ourselves apart from it, we begin at once to experience relief.

April 21

When we write, we "place" ourselves in our world. We say, "This is where I am, right now, and this is how I feel about that." Conversely, when we focus on the places where we have been, we often connect to a deep and specific sense of how we felt when we were there. In other words, by mapping our literal, physical placements, we are often able to more accurately map our psychological placement. Good writers know this.

April 22

We carry wisdom in our bodies. We carry memories and we carry, too, the medicine for what ails us. We can walk our way to sanity. We can walk our way to clarity. Baffled and confused, we can walk our way to knowing the "next right step." In difficult times, many of us intuitively start walking. We may walk our way through a divorce, a breakup, or a job change. We may walk our way out of one identity and into another, newer and better-suited to us. Answers come to us while we walk—sometimes the answers come to us before the questions. We just get an itch to start walking and when we do, we then begin to get a sense of why.

April 23

Drama in our lives often keeps us from putting drama on the page. Some drama happens and we lose our sense of scale in our emotional landscape. When this happens, we need to reconnect to our emotional through line. We need a sense of our "before, during, and after life."

April 24

Observed closely enough, all of life is interesting. The practice of writing teaches this. All of life is filled with drama. Observed closely, small moments have large impact. They are like the small variations as we move scale to scale in piano practice. The eye, like the ear, becomes trained to nuance by consistent attention. When we practice the art of close observation, we gain an emotional palette that has more shades, more possibilities, than the screaming extremes of black and white headlines declaring catastrophe and crisis.

April 25

All artists suffer doubts. Great directors watch from the back of screening rooms and have to breathe their hyperventilated doubt into brown paper bags. Brilliant actresses suffer stage fright as painful as rickets. Doubt is a part of the territory as an artist. Surviving doubt, learning to discern what is emotional terrorism and what is a proper, suggested course adjustment, is something an artist becomes more skilled at over time— and often only with the help of his creative elders who have suffered doubt themselves. We need faith to survive doubt and we also need charity. When doubt attacks, we must be vigilantly self-loving. The dark night of the soul comes to all artists. When it comes to you, know that it is simply a tricky part of the trail and that you will see better in the morning.

April 26

I believe that what we want to write wants to be written. I believe that as I have an impulse to create, the something I want to create has an impulse to want to be born. My job, then, is to show up on the page and let that something move through me. In a sense, what wants to be written is none of my business.

April 27

Acting our way into right thinking is putting pen to the page even when the censor is shrieking. It is choosing to write even when writing feels "wrong" to us—because we're tired, we're bothered, we're any number of things that writing will change if only we will let it. Doing it all the time, whether or not we are in the mood, gives us ownership of our writing ability. It takes it out of the realm of conjuring and makes it something as do-able as picking up a hammer and pounding a nail.

April 28

Perhaps the greatest barrier for any of us as we look for an expanded life is our own deeply held skepticism. This might be called *the secret doubt*. It does not seem to matter whether we are officially believers or agnostics. We have our doubts about all of this creator/creativity stuff, and those doubts are very powerful. Unless we air them, they can sabotage us. Many times, in trying to be good sports we stuff our feelings of doubt. We need to stop doing that and explore them instead.

April 29

In order for us to go forward, we must live in the now. We must take the day that we have been given and make of it what we can. We cannot change the past. We can only regret it, and such dwelling leaches optimism from the day at hand. It is one more way to be blocked and a sadly effective one—if only . . . If only things were different, but they're not!

April 30

Creatively, I am a creature of habit. My daily habits form the grid that I must cling to right now. I need to do a few simple things and to keep doing them. I do my Morning Pages. I take my Artist Dates. I walk. Whenever I fall off my simple grid, it is quite a tumble. Whenever I pick up the first doubt and allow that doubt to spiral me deep into despair, I need my basics to get me emotionally sober again. And so, I needed to get a typewriter and I needed to roll a piece of paper into the machine. I needed to have the tactile reassurance of a book unfolding, and unfolding a page at a time in an old-fashioned and orderly way. One day at a time, one page at a time. This is what I can live with.

MAY

May 1

The lilies of the field began as buds. We are asked to trust that just as they had a glorious and safe unfolding, so will we. In the natural world, we see butterflies emerge from awkward yet protective cocoons. We must remind ourselves to trust that sometimes we, too, are being protected in our growth. Our erraticism, our ungainliness, our panic—these, too, are natural to the passage of change. The Great Creator experiences all his creation in the throes of shifting identity. The unfolding saga of life on all levels is one of constant transformation, constant changing of form. When we cooperate with our need and desire to grow, we are cooperating with spiritual law.

May 2

Perfectionism is a refusal to let yourself move ahead. It is a loop—an obsessive, debilitating closed system that causes you to get stuck in the details of what you are writing or painting or making and to lose sight of the whole. Instead of creating feely and allowing errors to reveal themselves later as insights, we often get mired in getting the details right. We correct our originality into a uniformity that lacks passion and spontaneity. "Do not fear mistakes," Miles Davis told us. "There are none."

May 3

For those of us working to increase our creativity, it is always good to be out and about, especially on our feet. Walking, the simplest of tools, is among the most profound. It makes us larger than we are. When we walk, we wake up our consciousness. We enliven our senses. We arrive at a sense of well-being. We experience "conscious contact" with a power greater than ourselves. That still, small voice is automatically amplified a footfall at a time. *"Solvitur ambulando,"* St. Augustine of Hippo is said to have remarked. "It is solved by walking."

May 4

Festivity breeds creativity. Rigidity breeds despair. When our high spirits are straitjacketed in the name of virtue or discipline, the vital and youthful spark in us that enjoys adventure and is game for invention begins to flicker like a flame in a draft. Creativity responds to nourishment and warmth. If we are forbidden to be childlike— told perhaps that it is "childish" or "selfish"—if we are urged to be too sensible, we react as gifted students do to an authoritarian teacher—we refuse to learn and grow. Our considerable energy is channeled into resistance and over time solidified into a hard-to-penetrate shell of feigned indifference. The universe is alive with energy. It is fertile, abundant, even raucous—so are we. Most of us are high-spirited, humorous, even pranksterish with the least encouragement. What is lacking for so many of us is precisely the least encouragement.

May 5

Very often a risk is worth taking simply for the sake of taking it. There is something enlivening about expanding our self-definition, and a risk does exactly that. Selecting a challenge and meeting it creates a sense of self-empowerment that becomes the ground for further successful challenges. Viewed this way, running a marathon increases your chances of writing a full-length play. Writing a full-length play gives you a leg up on a marathon. Complete the following sentence. "If I didn't have to do it perfectly, I would try_____."

May 6

Artists love other artists. Shadow artists are gravitating to their rightful tribe but cannot yet claim their birthright. Very often audacity, not talent, makes one person an artist and another a shadow artist—hiding in the shadows, afraid to step out and expose the dream to the light, fearful that it will disintegrate to the touch. Shadow artists judge themselves harshly, beating themselves for years over the fact that they have not acted on their dreams. This cruelty only reinforces their status as shadow artists. Remember, it takes nurturing to make an artist. Shadow artists did not receive sufficient nurturing. They blame themselves for not acting fearlessly anyhow.

May 7

Art thrives on life. Life feeds it, enriches it, enlarges it. Cloistering ourselves away from life in the name of being artists causes us to run the risk of producing art that is arid, artless, and yes, heartless. For most artists, there is something risky about too much unstructured time, too much freedom to make nothing but art. We talk about self-expression, but we must develop a self to express. A self is developed not only alone, but in community. Day jobs help not only to pay the rent but also to build stamina and structure. Artists need both. A novel can be a vast savannah in which I wander alone—a musical may mean six years sailing across uncharted seas. Navigators need the stars to structure their voyages. We artists, too, need other points of reference to stay on course.

May 8

When we are rickety, Morning Pages lend us stability. They miniaturize the terrors that we are walking through. They bring life back down to the possible: Exactly what can we do today? Taken in a daily bite, most change, however extreme, can be metabolized. Our Pages give us time and place to get used to change. When we remember that we have a daily life, we begin to find our grounding. It is our job, faced with impending change, to continue to husband the life that we have got. It is our job to buy the kitty litter, call the plumber, keep our hand moving across the page.

May 9

Many recovering creatives sabotage themselves most frequently by making nice. There is a tremendous cost to such ersatz virtue. Many of us have made a virtue out of deprivation. We have embraced a long-suffering artistic anorexia as a martyr's cross. We have used it to feed a false sense of spirituality grounded in being good, meaning *superior*. Spirituality has often been misused as a route to an unloving solitude, a stance where we proclaim ourselves above our human nature. This spiritual superiority is really only one more form of denial. For an artist, virtue can be deadly. The urge toward respectability and maturity can be stultifying, even fatal.

May 10

As artists, we are perpetually seeking to penetrate the veil of cultural prescriptions and arrive at personal truth. In order to do this, we need to be brave enough with—and open enough to—our own internal territory that our art can express it. In other words, we must be able to face down shame and *choose* self-disclosure. This takes courage.

May 11

Writing, like jewelry design, is a series of choices that lead to a sense of something made—that something is "sense." Sense brings to the writer choice and, with choice, a sense of at least the potential for happiness.

May 12

I think if we talked more realistically about what creativity feels like, we might let ourselves do a little more of it. If we thought of it as normal—98.6 on the human spectrum—instead of a sudden spike in our psychic temperature, we might let ourselves do it as a daily practice. We might all show up at the page or the easel and discover that there are reams of work waiting to move through us, right now, in the exact life that we have already. We might discover that creativity is not a marathon event that we must gird ourselves for, whacking off great swaths of life as we know it to make room for it. Creativity is not aberrant, not dramatic, not dangerous. If anything, it is the pent-up energy of *not* using creativity that feels that way.

May 13

Art may be the finest form of prayer. Making art is quite literally a path "to our Maker." In the act of creation, the creator reveals himself or itself to us and we, too, are revealed to ourselves as something of the divine spark from which we ourselves are made. It is this primal fact of connection, artist to artist, Great Creator to us as creator, that the truest sense of our own identity is born. We make art not merely to make our way in the world but also to make something of ourselves, and often the something that we make is a person with an inviolable sense of inner dignity. We have answered yes when our true name was called.

May 14

Many of us are operating out of the toxic old idea that God's will for us and our will for us are at opposite ends of the table. "I want to be an actress, but God wants me to wait tables in hash joints," the scenario goes. "So if I try to be an actress, I will end up slinging hash." Thinking like this is grounded in the idea that God is a stern parent with very rigid ideas about what's appropriate for us. And you'd better believe we won't like them. This stunted god concept needs alteration. What would a nontoxic god think of your creative goals? Might such a god really exist?

May 15

It is spiritual law that the good of our projects and our growth as artists must rest in divine hands and not merely human ones. While we are led to and drawn from teacher to teacher, opportunity to opportunity, the Great Creator remains the ultimate source of all of our creative good. It is easy to forget this and make our agent or our manager or our current teacher the source of our "good." When we place our reliance on an undergirding of divine assistance, we are able to hear our cues clearly, thank those who step forward to aid us, release those who seem to impede us, and keep unfolding as artists with the faith that the Great Artist knows precisely what is best for us and can help us find our path, no matter how lost, distanced, or removed we may sometimes feel from our dream. In the heart of God, all things are close at hand, and this means our creative help, support, and success. As we ask, believe, and are open to receive, we are gently led.

May 16

If you feel stuck in your life or in your art, few jump-starts are more effective than a week of *reading deprivation*. No reading? That's right: no reading. It is a paradox that by emptying our lives of distractions we are actually filling the well. Without distractions, we are once again thrust into the sensory world. With no newspaper to shield us, a train becomes a viewing gallery. With no novel to sink into (and no television to numb us out) an evening becomes a vast savannah in which furniture—and other assumptions—get rearranged. We are cast into our inner silence. Our reward will be a new outflow. Our own art, our own thoughts and feelings, will begin to nudge aside the sludge of blockage, to loosen it and move it upward and outward until once again our well is running freely.

May 17

Work is the best antidote for savaged work. If we are engaged in making something new, we are less invested in the reception of something old. If we remember to keep our own counsel—"How did I like the work?"—then we are less likely to be blown apart by the judgment of others. Having a healthy forum of before, during, and after friends is also an enormous help. We need those who love us and our work for the long haul and not for a hot-off-the-presses pick or pan.

May 18

When we have an obsessive fear, we hold on to it like a dog with a bone. We cling to the thought with a die-hard intensity, nothing can pry us loose. It is a mantra we repeat to ourselves, "I am afraid that X is going to happen." Afraid of X, we fail to notice Y. We are fixated and, in our fixation, we feel trapped. We are never trapped. There are always choices. We do have freedom of will and movement and we can exercise them. We can find a small way to move forward and pry open the jaws of our trap. It is a question of being open-minded, but when our mind is trained on the bone, nothing can help us. This is when we must learn to let go and let God.

May 19

One of the biggest myths around writing is that in order to do it we must have great swathes of uninterrupted time. Speaking for myself, I have never had such silken bolts of time. The myth that we must have "time"—more time—in order to create is a myth that keeps us from using the time we do have. If we are forever yearning for "more," we are forever discounting what is offered.

May 20

For so many of us, it is hard to be both large enough and small enough to hold the range of life. Without a spiritual connection to something larger than ourselves, we lose our bearings, our beings, our sense of scale. Of course we do. The human experience is intricate, painful, and very beautiful. We lead lives filled with loss and filled with gain. Without a tool to metabolize what we live through—and for me that tool is Morning Pages—and even with it, it is hard to process who we have been and who we have become.

May 21

Owning something also means owning up to some-thing. It means accepting responsibility, which means, literally, response-ability. When we write about our lives we respond to them. As we respond to them we are rendered more fluid, more centered, more agile on our own behalf. We are rendered conscious. Each day, each life, is a series of choices, and as we use the lens of writing to view our lives, we see our choices.

May 22

Most of the time when we are blocked in an area of our life, it is because we feel safer that way. We may not be happy, but at least we know what we are—unhappy. Much fear of our own creativity is the fear of the unknown. If I am fully creative, what will it mean? What will happen to me and to others? We have some pretty awful notions about what *could* happen. So, rather than find out, we decide to stay blocked.

May 23

Morning Pages remind me that while I cannot choose much of what happens to me in my life, I can choose how I respond to what happens. The trick is getting small enough to inch forward. The past is huge. The future may be huge as well. What remains for me, what is given, is to do the small tasks of the day. First among those tasks is Morning Pages, the daily writing of three pages that draws me into the life I have now, the choices I can make today to find beauty in what is given to me.

May 24

When we are willing to make what wants to be made rather than make what we want, we become open to new directions. We begin to be able to let some of the seriousness out of our artist's life, and we begin to let some of the playfulness back in. It is an ironic fact that most great artists are inherently playful.

May 25

Writing is like breathing. I believe that. I believe we all come into life as writers. We are born with a gift for language and it comes to us within months as we begin to name our world. We all have a sense of ownership, a sense of satisfaction as we name objects that we find. Words give us power.

May 26

At its essence, art *is* an alchemical process. By practicing art, by living artfully, we realize our vein of gold. What I refer to as "the vein of gold," Egyptians referred to as "the golden ray." It is the individual, indisputable, indestructible connection to the divine. The vein of gold in every life is located in the heart of that life. The heart is the origin of creative impulses.

May 27

Accidents happen, and when they do and we are willing to roll with the punches, our creativity springs up and takes a turn. "Just let me see what I can make from this," the inner creator says. "There must be a silk purse in here somewhere." When we are willing to be open-minded, silk purses abound.

May 28

So much of being sane and happy begins with the doing of things that are sane and happy. This means that we must train ourselves to think small rather than large. We become frightened because we have "big decisions" to make. But big decisions can be made gently, a small step at a time. But again, notice that word in there—"step." Walking leads us a step at a time. Walking gives us a gentle path. We are talked to as we walk. We hear guidance. It comes from within us and from the world around us. Walking is a potent form of prayer. "Guide me, show me," we pray as we walk, and as we walk we are guided and we are shown.

May 29

When we are unable to work, we can work at the work of getting ready to work. Writers can lay in supplies of paper and enticing pens, notepads that plead "Please write on me." Painters can prepare their canvases, clean their brushes, neaten their studio space. Potters can acquire a new lump of cool clay and clear the table space where they will knead and shape it. Gentle things can be done.

May 30

When I am in a period of drought, my chief enemy is despair. I am afraid to harbor hope, and yet it is the gentle harboring of hope that is the antidote to dryness of the spirit. In arid times we must practice a very gentle discipline. We must keep on keeping on. Morning Pages are never more important than in those periods when we seek to eke them onto the page a drop at a time. The slightest trickle, the merest hint of water, creative juice, is what we are after.

May 31

I would disagree with those who say we cannot change the past. We can heal it, transform it, utilize it, build on it—any number of creative things.

JUNE

June 1

As recovering creatives, many of us find that every time our career heats up we reach for our nearest Wet Blanket. We blurt out our enthusiasm to our most skeptical friend—in fact, we call him up. If we don't, he calls us. This is the Test. Our artist is a child, an inner youngster, and when he/she is scared, Mommy is what's called for. Unfortunately, many of us have Wet Blanket mommies and a whole army of Wet Blanket surrogate mommies—those friends who have our second, third, and fourth thoughts for us. The trick is not to let them be that way. How? *Zip the lip. Button up. Keep a lid on it. Don't give away the gold.* Always remember: the first rule of magic is self-containment. You must hold your intention within yourself, stoking it with power. Only then will you be able to manifest what you desire.

June 2

It is my belief that all of us are naturally intuitive and that writing opens an inner spiritual doorway that gives us access to information both personally and professionally that serves us well. I call this information "guidance," lacking another word and not feeling, since it now seems so normal and matter-of-fact, that "ESP" is the term that best applies. An open mind, a spirit of scientific inquiry, and the willingness to delve into the unknown can lead all writers to an unexpected inner resource that will greatly enrich both their lives and their work. This is not my theory. It is my objective experience.

June 3

For those of us who have become artistically anorectic—yearning to be creative and refusing to feed that hunger in ourselves so that we become more and more focused on our deprivation—a little authentic luxury can go a long way. The key word here is *authentic*. Because art is born in expansion, in a belief in sufficient supply, it is critical that we pamper ourselves for the sense of abundance it brings to us. All too often, we become blocked and blame it on our lack of money. This is *never* an authentic block. The actual block is our feeling of constriction, our sense of powerlessness. Art requires us to empower ourselves with choice. At the most basic level, this means choosing to do self-care.

June 4

As artists, we wish we could always work well, but we must settle for working always. The "always" we can control. The "well" we cannot control. For this reason, we do well to simply serve, to focus more on the process of doing our work than on the "product" of work produced.

June 5

We often make the mistake of thinking that we "have" to be in the "right" mood to write. The truth is, any mood can be used for writing. Any mood is a good writing mood. The trick is to simply enter whatever mood like a room and sit down and write from there.

June 6

There is one divine mind working through all and in all. When we consciously acknowledge that fact and ask that our own dreams and projects be manifested as part of the diving unfolding, then we are on the right track. We are open again to mystery as well as mastery. We are taking our proper place as a creation amid creation, a divine idea that continues divine thought by plans and projects of our own. Our will and God's will are not inimical. Our dreams and God's dream for us are not so different. In fact, our heart's dream and the dream of God may be the same. We can hope so, and in our hope we can trust that our dreams will be fulfilled.

June 7

It is so easy to rush ahead into fear and panic. It is so easy to miss the beauty that awaits us in the here and now. The tiniest things can bring joy. So much of life is like taking a photograph. We must pause to catch the moment and savor our delight. Savoring the moment is a learned art, and it is an art that must be practiced to be perfected. The mother must notice the pink blossoms and think to bring her camera. Her child is growing up, growing up daily, and the seasons of his life will come only once. This spring Sunday is worth capturing.

June 8

You may want to remind yourself that "art" is a form of the verb "to be." Many of us have the idea that there's such a thing as a real artist, and "one day we may be one." My feeling is that if you are making art, you are already a real artist. Over time, you may become a better one, more skilled in your craft, but what do real artists do? They make art. If you're making art, even beginning art, you are a real artist—at least today. And the day, the process of days adding up and experience adding up, is all we have for sure. So give yourself credit.

June 9

Writing is alchemy. Writing that poem, moving out of the cramped and cerebral space of bitterness into the capacious heart, I am no longer a victim, an enemy, an injured party. I am what I am again: a writer. Writing is medicine. It is an appropriate antidote to injury. It is an appropriate companion for any difficult change. Writing about the change, we can help it along, lean into it, cooperate. Writing allows us to rewrite our lives.

June 10

Our creativity never leaves us. Sometimes, however, its surface appearance fades away. We become parched with longing for our work, but our sources of strength are now not our easy tricks. We are being humbled and opened for greater work to come through us, and that humility feels to us like humiliation, that opening-up feels like a gaping wound. We are deathly afraid that art has left us alone forever, that we will never see the beloved's face or feel its simple touch. "I was such a fool," we think. "I took so much for granted." And we did. But faced with our drought, we don't any longer, and this is the beginning of humility and honesty. It is the beginning of emptying ourselves so art can again pour through us.

June 11

Attitudes are what determine our spiritual altitude. If we are mired in resentment, fear, and animosity, we will interpret events and people through that negative filter. Once we have done that, we will act—actually, re-act—accordingly. The burden of bad attitudes weighs us down. On a creative pilgrimage we cannot afford them. It is our attitude that allows us to view difficulties as lessons or opportunities, challenges instead of setbacks.

June 12

When we are angry at being overlooked, it is not arrogance and grandiosity. It is a signal that we have changed sizes and must now act larger. Very often when we feel small and unheard, it is not because we *are* small and unheard but because we are acting small and unheard. We are not intended to be small. Often we are cornered not into being powerless and puny—as we feel—but into being large. Our problem is our perspective. When we are angry "out of all proportion," that is a very accurate phrase. We have lost a sense of our true size and power, and the intensity of our feelings makes us feel "hopping mad," another telling phrase, as our mental image of ourselves becomes very cartooned. The size of our anger has dwarfed our perspective and our personality. This is because we do not realize that the power we are perceiving is within us as the power for change. When we feel impotent with rage, we are actually potent with rage—we simply have not yet seen how to effectively use our anger as the fuel that it is.

June 13

Writing from the body—dropping down into the well of your experience and sounding out how you feel—ultimately yields a body of work. We say that a voice is full-bodied without realizing that this is a literal phrase: when we write from our gut rather than from our head we acquire the same resonance that a singer does when the breath comes from the diaphragm rather than high up in the chest.

June 14

Whenever you feel stymied, stuck, or frantic, remind yourself, this is the result of having too many good ideas—even if it feels like you have no good ideas at all. The trick is to establish a gentle flow, to keep that gentle flow trickling forward. This keeps the dammed-up ideas from bursting through and flooding you. Remember, creativity is not fickle, finite, or limited. There are always ideas. Good ideas. Workable ideas, brave and revolutionary ideas. Calm and serviceable ideas. The trick is to gently access them and allow them to flow. In other words, it's time for that 12-Step adage "Easy does it," because the truth is, easy *does* do it, and frantic, forced, and frenetic does not.

June 15

We are not alone and unpartnered in our desire to make art. Art is an act of expansion and faith. We are the children of an expansive power that interacts with us when we act on faith. When we are open to good things, good things come to us. Sometimes, in order for something good to happen, something apparently bad must happen first. This is when we are asked to have faith. This is when we are required to search for the silver lining. Our dreams may feel thwarted when in reality they are being tempered. We are being shaped to fit a divine purpose. We can cooperate or we can resist.

June 16

When we focus on process, our creative life retains a sense of adventure. Focused on product, the same creative life can feel foolish or barren. We inherit the obsession with product and the idea that art produces finished product from our consumer-oriented society. This focus creates a great deal of creative block. We, as working artists, may want to explore a new artistic area, but we don't see where it will get us. We wonder if it will be good for our career. Fixated on the need to have something to show for our labors, we often deny our curiosities. Every time we do this, we are blocked. The grace to be a beginner is always the best prayer for an artist. The beginner's humility and openness lead to exploration. Exploration leads to accomplishment. All of it begins at the beginning, with the first small and scary step.

June 17

Whether we call it reaching for God or reaching for the Muse, there is a humility to be found in the making of art. We strive to make what wants to be made. We open ourselves to inspiration and as we do so, we are led. We do not always *feel* that we are being led. We must affirm it in the face of our own doubt. We must go forward acting "as if." When we are willing to do that, we get a sense of our place in the greater scheme of things.

June 18

*M*orning Pages are nonnegotiable. They will teach you that your mood doesn't really matter. Some of the best creative work gets done on the days when you feel that everything you're doing is just plain junk. The Morning Pages will teach you to stop judging and just let yourself write. So what if you're tired, crabby, distracted, stressed? Your artist is a child and it needs to be fed. Morning Pages feed your artist child. So write your Morning Pages.

June 19

There is room for art in any life we have—any life, no matter how crowded or overstuffed, no matter how arid or empty. We are the "block" we perceive. If you are a beginning musician and want to learn piano, sit down at the piano and touch the keys. Great. Tomorrow you can sit down at the piano and touch the keys again. Five minutes a day is better than no minutes a day. Five minutes might lead to ten, just as a tentative embrace leads to something more passionate. Making art is making love with life. We open ourselves to art as to love. Instead of thinking about conquering an art form, think instead of kissing it hello, wooing it, exploring it in small, enticing steps. How many of us have burned through promising relationships by moving too swiftly? How many of us have burned out in new creative ventures by setting goals too high? Most of us.

June 20

Jealousy is a map. Each of our jealousy maps differs. Each of us will probably be surprised by some of the things we discover on our own. Jealousy is always a mask for fear: fear that we aren't able to get what we want; frustration that somebody else seems to be getting what is rightfully ours even if we are too frightened to reach for it. At its root, jealousy is a stingy emotion. It doesn't allow for the abundance and multiplicity of the universe. Jealousy tells us there is room for only one—one poet, one painter, one whatever you dream of being. The truth, revealed by action in the direction of our dreams, is that there is room for all of us.

June 21

Creativity flourishes when we have a sense of safety and self-acceptance. Your artist, like a small child, is happiest when feeling a sense of security. As our artist's protective parent, we must learn to place our artist with safe companions. Toxic playmates can capsize our artist's growth.

June 22

Center stage belongs to those who are willing to move there, some talented and some not. Rather than angrily decrying the behavior and lack of talent of the "arrogant spotlight-grabbers," we need to use our anger to turn our own voltage up a little despite our fears. We need to say our own names as artists. When we do, we feel self-respect. Self-respect comes from the Self. The market will say what it will, but we need to say our own name as artists. When we complain that others do not take ourselves and our values seriously, we are actually saying that *we* don't. If our aesthetics matter so much to us, we must act on them in a concrete and specific form.

June 23

When we are willing to be open-minded, art and beauty come flooding into us in a thousand small ways. When we let ourselves see the possibilities instead of the improbabilities, we become as flexible and resilient as we really are. It is human nature to create. When we cooperate with our creativity, using it to live within the lives we actually have, we surprise ourselves with our level of invention. The closing medley becomes the opening medley. Today's snatched sentence opens the new play.

June 24

The heart of creativity is an experience of the mystical union; the heart of the mystical union is an experience of creativity. Those who speak in spiritual terms routinely refer to God as the creator but seldom see *creator* as the literal term for *artist*. I am suggesting you take the term *creator* quite literally. You are seeking to forge a creative alliance, artist-to-artist with the Great Creator. Accepting this concept can greatly expand your creative possibilities.

June 25

We have to suffer for our art, right?" my writer friend asked me.

I believe that if we believe that, we surely will suffer. We may not even notice when we are not. In my experience, it is not the act of making art that is painful. It is the desire to make something and not acting on it that causes pain. When we are engaged in our creativity, we are in love with our process. Yes, there may be stretches where the going gets rough, but that happens in any love affair. To my eye, what is really painful is *not* practicing our creativity.

June 26

Reality happens in daily doses. Life lived a day at a time is life made much of. It is not that we cannot see the larger picture or that we do not need to acknowledge the larger movements in our life, but movements in life, as in a symphony, are made from myriad tiny notes, each one a point of consciousness. Writing to ourselves, we are taking note as to the notes we are playing. We are hearing ourselves as we sing our song. We are able, then, to be instrumental in our own change. We become not merely players but conductors/composers as well.

June 27

Creativity involves process, and process involves change. The truism we often hear is that we often resist change because change is difficult or change is painful. This is not quite accurate. It is the *resistance* to change that is difficult or painful. In the same way, *it is the resistance to our creativity that causes us to equate it with suffering. It is important to remember that "effort" and "suffering" are two different things.*

June 28

In any creative life there are dry seasons. These droughts appear from nowhere and stretch to the horizon like a Death Valley vista. Life loses its sweetness; our work feels mechanical, empty, forced. We feel we have nothing to say, and we are tempted to say nothing. During a drought, we are fighting with God. We have lost faith—in the Great Creator and in our creative selves. We have some bone to pick, and bones to pick are everywhere. These are the times when the Morning Pages are most difficult and most valuable. During a drought, the mere act of showing up on the page, like the act of walking through a track-less desert, requires one footfall after another to no apparent point. *Droughts do end*. Droughts end because we have kept writing our pages. They end because we have not collapsed to the floor of our despair and refused to move. In a creative life, droughts are a necessity. The time in the *desert* brings us clarity and charity. When you are in the drought, know that it is to a purpose. And keep writing Morning Pages.

June 29

Our life is supposed to be our life and our art is supposed to be something we do *in* it and with it. Our life must be larger than our art. It must be the container that holds it. Life is not linear. Our Artist's Way is a long and winding road, and we travel it best in the company of others, engaged not in the inner movie of the ego but in the outer-directed attention that fills the well with images and stocks the imagination with stories. Rather than yearning to be "full-time artists," we might aspire to being full-time humans. When we do, art is the overflow of a heart filled with life.

June 30

Great art lies not in the generic but in the specific. It lies not in "more or less"—as we lamely conclude a thought to a bored listener—but in "exactly like this!" as we excitedly show or tell someone perceptive. A tepid ear, a hurried glance, a lack of real focus—these can chill and even destroy an early work and a fragile worker. Yes, artists are resilient, but we are also like tender shoots. Our thoughts and our ideas must be welcomed or, like shy suitors, they get discouraged and go away.

JULY

July 1

When we make the art we love, it makes time and energy available to us for our professional pursuits. Why? Because we feel more vital, and that vitality is assertive energy that makes room for its own desires. When we say, "I will articulate my true values, I will express my essence," that word "will" throws a switch. When we "will," then we "will." In this sense we are predicting our future and shaping it simultaneously. Everything is energy. Ideas are simply organized energy, a sort of mold into which more solidified energy can be poured. A book begins as an idea. So does a social movement. So does a building. We cast our dreams and desires ahead of us, and as we move toward them, their content takes on solidity. We cocreate our lives. This is both our responsibility and our privilege. Commit to make something you love and you will find that the needed supplies come to hand. Our creative energy triggers a creative response.

July 2

Dreams come to us from a divine source. If we follow them, they lead us back to a divine source. When we work toward our dreams, we are working toward our God. In reaching for guidance about our dreams, we are reaching toward God. Our dreams are not futile. They do not spring from our egos. They have their roots in our souls. Dreams must be guarded like children. Like children, they must be nurtured and soothed.

July 3

Early in my writing life, I tried to polish as I went. Each sentence, each paragraph, each page, had to flow from and build on what went before it. I thought a lot about all of this. I really worked at it. The danger of writing and rewriting at the same time was that it was tied in to my mood. In an expansive mood, whatever I wrote was great. In a constricted mood, nothing was good. This made writing a roller coaster of judgment and indictment: guilty or innocent, good or bad. I wanted a saner, less extreme way to write than this. I wanted emotional sobriety in my writing. I learned to write setting judgment aside and save a polish for later. I gave myself emotional permission to do rough drafts and for those rough drafts to be, well, rough. Freed to be rough, my writing actually became smoother. Freed from the demand that it be instantly brilliant, my writing became not only smoother but also easier and more clear.

July 4

It is no coincidence that artistic annals are filled with tales of incendiary romantic intrigues, yielding blazing creative work. Our muses *are* fuse-lighters, and the blaze they ignite may be passionate, creative, or both. Artists can marry, but they must marry well. And, I would argue, there must be *merriment* in their marriage for their work to continue to flourish. In artist-to-artist relationships, *both* artists need to be nurtured and seen. Neither partner should be neutered or neutralized by excessive caretaking. Agendas cannot replace adventures.

July 5

Creativity cannot be comfortably quantified in intellectual terms. By its very nature, creativity eschews such containment. In a university where the intellectual life is built upon the art of criticizing—on deconstructing a creative work—the art of creation itself, the art of creative construction, meets with scanty support, understanding, or approval. To be blunt, most academics know how to take something apart, but not how to assemble it. For an artist, to become overly cerebral is to become crippled. This is not to say that artists lack rigor; rather that artistic rigor is grounded differently than intellectual life usually admits.

July 6

There is something enlivening about writing in duos. A great deal of usable track can be laid in chummy proximity. So effective is propinquity at creating courage that Arts Anonymous, the twelve-step program dedicated to creative health, holds a once-weekly writing workshop, where members sit down side by side to attack their blocks on paper.

July 7

Waiting for art to be easy, we make it hard. We take our emotional temperature and find ourselves below normal, lacking in resolve. We would do it, we know we could do it, but we decide to wait until the doing of it is more effortless. In other words, we put ourselves in a passive position relative to our art. We want something outside of ourselves, the wind of inspiration, to blow our way and then we will get at it. The truth is that getting at it is what makes getting at it easier.

July 8

The process of creative emergence is a process of energy expansion. Wherever our energy is blocked by denial, the buried emotions and information need to be allowed to surface. Our original self seeks to break free so that our creative energies can move into expression. We are *not* cracking up under the pressure of self-exploration. Instead, we are cracking open a self-concept that has become confining and claustrophobic to our spirit.

July 9

Most droughts of the spirit occur because we have tried to be too self-sufficient. We have forgotten that our creativity is a spiritual gift with its taproot in Spirit and not in our own will. "Not I, but the father doeth the works," Christ told us. Great artists through the ages have insisted that they were merely channels for divine energy, that God worked through them, bringing their art to form. Feeling our connection to the divine, we feel less alone, less the sole architect of what it is we would accomplish.

July 10

Increasing and regularizing our times of solitude and quiet increases our ability to receive guidance. One way to think of it is that we are creating a sort of spiritual clearing. I have a centering song which goes:

In the center of your heart
Is a still small part,
Like a meadow in a forest made of green.
In the center of your heart,
Is a still small part,
And that is where your soul must go to dream.

In other words, we clear space in our lives in order to center and clear space in our hearts. The soul's voice, the voice of guidance, then ventures into the clearing we have created for it.

July 11

Mythologist Joseph Campbell advised those seeking fulfilling lives to follow their bliss. Nowhere is this better advice than in writing. When we choose to write about what we truly care about, when our values and the characters' values coincide, when our stakes and the story's stakes coincide, we write with passion, purity, and purpose. Like lightning bolts, we hit our target and shed some light in the process.

July 12

I believe we are creations of the Great Creator and that we are intended to be creative ourselves. I believe that when we humbly cooperate by making something every day, we are making something also out of ourselves, and it is a something that God intends for us—souls joyous and effective, active and self-actualized.

July 13

We are not meant to think of our creativity as some wild and savage beast caged in our subconscious. That's the part of the cultural mythology that has robbed us of our birthright as creative beings. No, the idea of being an artist isn't an act of ego. The ego wants us *not* to write or paint or dance or act—or to do that thing *perfectly.* That, of course, is impossible, and so often we are afraid to do it all. Our creativity is a normal and natural part of us. We are meant to sing, dance, draw, and doodle poems. Art lives in the *heart*, and we all have one.

July 14

As artists, we need people who can see us for who we are—as big as we are and as small as we are, as competent and powerful as we are, and as terrified and as tiny as we sometimes feel. As artists, we need people who believe in us and are able to see our large selves, and people who are able to be gentle and compassionate with our smaller selves. It is tremendously important to accurately distinguish who among our friends can accommodate each size.

July 15

Time is a primary concern in dealing with creative block. Most of us think, "If only I had more time, then I would work." We have a fantasy that there is such a thing as good creative time, an idyll of endless, seamless time unfolding invitingly for us to frolic in creatively. No such bolts of limitless time exist for most of us. Our days are chopped into segments, and if we are to be creative, we must learn to use the limited time we have.

July 16

When a writer writes from the heart of what matters to him personally, the writing is often both personal and powerful. When a writer writes to what he thinks the market needs—writes, in other words, without a personal investment—the standard of writing is often lowered along with the stakes. Part of our duty as writers is to do the work of honestly determining what matters to us and to try to write about that. This may take a certain amount of courage. This may mean that we do not meet with immediate support from those who make decisions with an eye to the market.

July 17

"Charity begins at home" is not a bromide. It is a direction. It means start with being nice to yourself, your authentic self, then try being nice to everyone else. When we place ourselves too low in the pecking order, we feel henpecked and, yes, we feel peckish. We neglect our work or do it distractedly. When we undervalue ourselves, we literally bury ourselves in lives not our own. Meeting the expectations of others, we may misplace our own values. Violating our true selves, we soon feel worthless and undeserving. As an artist, being nice is not nearly as important as being authentic. When we are what we truly are and say what we truly mean, we stop shouldering the responsibility for everyone else's shortfalls and become accountable to ourselves. When we do, astonishing shifts occur. We become aligned with our true higher power, and creative grace flows freely. When we stop playing God, God can play through us.

July 18

When we are in the midst of making something, in the actual creative act, we know we are who and what we are because we forget our public reception for a minute. We become the art itself instead of the artist who makes it. In the actual moment of making art, we are blessedly anonymous. Even when done in public, the act of making art is a private act. Creativity is always between us and our creative energy, us and the creative power working through us. When we are able to stay clearly and cleanly focused on that, then we are able to do very well.

July 19

Assumed in a believing-mirror relationship is the fact that it is God's will for us to use our talents. This in itself is radical. We have often been raised with a false sense of modesty. We have been taught it is better, somehow more spiritual, to be small not large. We have been tutored to hamper our own creative flight with doubts as to whether such flight is seemly. A believing mirror wants us to soar. To them, our bigger self is our true self, the self to aspire to. For a believing mirror, nothing is too good to be true. Spiritually grounded even if not conventionally religious, a believing mirror focuses on the divine spark of genius within us all. Because that divine spark is godly in origin, anything is possible. When we are connected to the Divine within us, nothing is beyond our reach.

July 20

So much of art hinges on our ability to trust intuition, to follow our hunch about what "might" or "could" come next. The difference between a blocked artist and a free one is this precise openness to moment-by-moment invention. Agnes de Mille tells us that an artist must take "leap after leap in the dark." Picasso tells us that we are all born children, "the trick is remaining one." How do we remain one? Having the time of our lives is the answer. Being open to the right timing of coincidence is the key.

July 21

As long as we can continue to deny the possibility of spiritual support for our endeavors, we can comfortably set a low ceiling on our dreams and goals. The phrase "I'd love to, but" can often be found smooching with the Yeah, But Syndrome. Spiritual experiences are, well, *spiri*tual experiences. They may feel weird. Some of us may feel self-conscious or frightened by them. If we can deny them, we can back off both from our spiritual support and our creative possibilities. Remember that the phrase "it would take a miracle" is often used to refuse to invite one.

July 22

Creativity is inspiration coupled with initiative. It is an act of faith and, in that phrase, the word "act" looms as large as the "faith" that it requires. When we do not act in the direction of our dreams, we are only "dreaming." Dreams coupled with the firm intention to manifest them take on a steely reality. Our dreams come true when we are true to them. Reality contains the word "real." We begin to "reel" in our dreams when we toss out the baited hook of intention. When we shift our inner statement from "I'd love to" to "I'm going to," we shift out of victim and into adventurer.

July 23

We like to believe we must make things happen. We also like to believe we can't. This means we can worry about our powerlessness and get steeped in our own bitterness. The truth is, we are meant to co-create. In other words, we both make things happen and let things happen; we imagine and then we release the imagined dream into the Universe for it to manifest it properly. Far from being powerless, we have all the power of the Universe available to us, if we will cooperate with it in its unfolding.

July 24

I have learned that if I take my artist on a date, it responds like any other sullen romantic interest. After a while, it stops sulking and it talks to me. It has ideas to share and so, like spatting lovers meeting "just for a moment," it shares a coquettish thought—just to get me interested. It asks a question that sets me to thinking, and soon, there we are, at it again.

July 25

There are many negative core beliefs about artists, yet none need be true. They come to us from our parents, our religion, our culture, and our fearful friends. Once we have cleared away the most sweeping cultural negatives, we may find we are still stubbornly left with core negatives we have acquired from our families, teachers, and friends. These are often more subtle—but equally undermining if not confronted. Our business is confronting them. Negative beliefs are exactly that: beliefs, not facts. You are not dumb, crazy, egomaniacal, grandiose, or silly just because you falsely believe yourself to be. *What you are is scared. Core negatives keep you scared.*

July 26

In periods of intense pain, I walk it out. In times of elation, when I can't embody my emotion properly, I walk it out. I walk to meditate and "hear," and I also walk to pray and "speak." It is on my long solitary walks that the Universe gets an earful from me and vice versa. Walks are the generators for me of what I call my "alpha ideas." These alpha ideas are the ideas that seem to come from a higher source than myself, suggesting better solutions to my creative or daily problems than my ordinary thinking does.

July 27

When we write from the inside out rather than the outside in, when we write about what most concerns us rather than about what we feel might sell, we often write so well and so persuasively that the market responds to our efforts. It is also true that when we see that the market exists for a topic that is high stakes for us, there is no dishonor in writing to that slice of the market. Then we are in the luxurious position of being able to write both from the inside out and from the outside in. It is only when we try writing from the outside in, writing on a topic that has stakes that are not personally compelling, that we run the risk of writing thinly and unpersuasively.

July 28

When we surrender to becoming what we are meant to be instead of trying to convince the world of who we think we are, we find our proper creative shoes and can walk in them comfortably. Not surprisingly, they sometimes take us far. Moving comfortably and at a less driven pace, we also enjoy the journey, finding pleasure in our companions and our "view" each step of the way.

July 29

When we trust ourselves, we become both more humble and more daring. When we trust ourselves, we move surely. There is no unnecessary strain in our grasp as we reach out to meet life. There is no snatching at people and events, trying to force them to give us what we think we want. We become what we are meant to be. It is that simple. We become what we are, and we do it by being who we are, not who we strive to be.

July 30

When we are blocked creatively, we often experience ourselves as miserable—and we then wonder, "How neurotic am I?" Thinking that therapy will supply that answer, or at least alleviate our misery, we often turn to therapy only to find that our misery continues unabated. Of course it does. We are miserable not because we are neurotic but because we are creative and not functioning in our creativity. Therapy may help us to "understand" our blocks. We do better to simply get over them. Art is therapeutic. It is *not* therapy. Therapy aims at transformation through understanding. Art aims at transformation more directly. When we make a piece of art about something we don't understand, we come to understand it, or, at least, our relationship to it through our own experience—which is more full-bodied than merely cerebral. In this sense, art "works" therapeutically whether we understand it or not.

July 31

As writers, care and maintenance of our writing muscles are necessary for our writing stamina. This means that we must take the time and attention necessary to fill the well instead of drawing on it unrelentingly and without consciousness of our inner limits. While this may sound difficult or onerous, the payoff in terms of our writing lives is enormous. Even the smallest amount of self-nurturance will have an immediate and beneficial impact on our writing. A regular and gentle program of self-care will result in a level of ease and authority in our writing that is often astounding.

AUGUST

August 1

As artists, we do much better trying to keep things simple. We do better to compare ourselves solely to ourselves. Self-inventory is useful, while self-flagellation is not. Without calling our whole identity into question, there are inquiries that we can fruitfully ask. How am I developing as an artist? Am I doing the work necessary for me to mature? Did I work today? Yes? Well, that's good. Working today is what gives us currency and self-respect. It is what cannot be taken away from us. There is dignity in work.

August 2

Writing is about living. It is about specificity. Writing is about seeing, hearing, feeling, smelling, touching. It is more about all these things than it is about thinking. I believe in specificity. I trust it. Specificity is like breathing: one breath at a time, that is how life is built. One thing at a time, one thought, one word at a time. That is how a writing life is built.

August 3

When the student is willing, the teacher appears, spiritual sages tell us. Another way to put it is that when we are willing to be taught, we become teachable. We always move ahead in our art when we open our heart to willingness. In order to do something well, we must first be willing to do it badly. We must have the humility to be once again a beginner, to admit what we don't know and admit that we wish to know more.

August 4

A primary reason writers procrastinate is in order to build up a sense of deadline. Deadlines create a flow of adrenaline. Adrenaline medicates and overwhelms the censor. Writers procrastinate so that when they finally get to writing, they can get past the censor.

August 5

I don't know why it is that we fail to talk about art in terms of humble diligence. So much of making a career as an artist consists of the small strokes, the willingness to show up and try on a daily basis. So much of being good at something consists of being practiced at something so that the sudden gusts of a deadline blowing into your work space doesn't turn you into a terrorist, wild-haired and wild-eyed, unable to muster muscle and nerve enough to simply stick to the page. As artists, we can make our work daily and doable enough that we give it its daily measure of time and consistency. We can "show up" for our artist and, if we do, when we call on it, our artist will show up for us.

August 6

Art moves through us. It is colored by our individuality, but we are not precisely its origin. Or, to put it differently, a piece of art may originate with us, but we originate somewhere larger ourselves. We are, each of us, more than we seem, more than the sum of our merely human components. There is a divine spark animating each of us, and that divine spark also animates our art. When we dedicate a piece of art to something larger than our ego, that something larger becomes a felt presence. There is a breath of the divine that blows through us as artists and blows through our art as well.

August 7

Over the years, I have learned that there is a flow of ideas that we as artists can tap into. The flow of creativity is a constant. We are the ones who are fickle or fearful. I have learned that my creative condition and my spiritual condition are one and the same. Making art is an act of faith, a movement toward expansion. When I am stymied in my work, I am stymied in my spiritual condition. When I am self-conscious as an artist, I am spiritually constricted. I need to pray to lose my self-centered fears. I need to ask for selflessness, to be a conduit, a channel for ideas to move through.

August 8

For all of us, it is a delicate dance knowing when to be stubborn in our knowing and when to be open to input and others' knowing. We cannot make art by consensus. On the other hand, we do not always need to lead, to inaugurate, and to initiate. Having done that, having laid the track out of a first draft, we have to be open to input and improvement, and it may come to us, as mine currently does, in the form of other experts commenting from their strengths with no agendas of their own except good work.

August 9

All actions require creative energy. As artists, we must learn to think of our energy the way a person thinks about money—am I spending my energy wisely here, investing in this person, this situation, this use of my time? As a rule, artists are temperamentally generous, even spendthrift. This natural inclination must be consciously monitored. An artist must return enough to the inner well to feel a sense of well-being.

August 10

If your head is awhirl and you "cannot think straight," then start by straightening something up. Fold your laundry. Sort your drawers. Go through your closet and hang things more neatly. Straighten your bed. Go get the lemon Pledge and dust and shine your bookcase and your dresser—often, when we are engaged in such small, homely tasks, a sense of being "at home" will steal over us. When we take the time to husband the details of our lives, we may encounter a sense of grace. In 12-Step slang, "God" has often been said to stand for "Good Orderly Direction." Often, in making a sense of order, we encounter a direction we can valuably express ourselves in.

August 11

So much of being an artist involves that Nike slogan, "Just do it." So much good comes from our just showing up. Of course it is seductive, the idea that we will one day be in the mood, and we will work that day like a "real" artist. But a great deal of real art is made under the radar. We barely know we are working. We just suit up and show up and grab what moments we can, and it is only in cozy retrospect that we see the level of skill we were able to muster. It is humbling, the degree to which we are like automatons. Our art moves through us despite us.

August 12

There is a tension, an excitement, a spark of possibility in all great conversation. If writing is a conversation with life, then we must bring to that conversation our alert attention, our willingness to be surprised. We must bring our writer's world an open eye, an eye that is focused on the world around us and not merely on the inner world of our own concerns. Writing rewards practice. Writing rewards attention. Writing, like sex with the right partner, remains a gateway to greater mystery, a way to touch something greater than ourself. Writing is an act of cherishing. It is an act of love.

August 13

One of the pivotal problems in creative growth is the question of accurate self-assessment. How do we know how large we can be if we don't know how large we are? Frightened of being bigheaded and egotistical, we seldom ask, "Am I being too limited, too small for who I really am?" Expansion can be frightening. Growth can feel foreign, even "wrong." As artists, we may experience shifts in size as hallucinogenic events, like Alice after she ate the mushroom. One day we feel very large and competent. The next day we will feel that yesterday's grander size was just grandiosity and that we are really much smaller and more wobbly than we knew. Changing sizes, we go through growing pains, and many of those pains are the pangs of an identity crisis. We may pray about it only to discover prayer is no help: God himself seems to be forging our new identity. The more we pray for it to go away, the stronger it actually becomes.

August 14

So often as artists the blocks that we feel to be ours alone can be dissolved by being shared. We have the opportunity to help one another and when we are willing to take it, great things can come to pass. So much of making art is like running a marathon. We may have to run the race ourselves but it is tremendously helpful to have friends who can cheer us on.

August 15

There seems to be an unwritten spiritual law that if we want our good to increase, we must focus on appreciating and husbanding the good that we already experience. This can be done by writing gratitude lists enumerating the many things in our current life that are fruitful and rewarding. On a concrete level, it can be done by the careful husbanding of what we have. This means that buttons get sewn on, hems get tacked up, smudges get scrubbed off doorjambs. We make the very best of exactly what we have and we find that almost behind our back the Great Creator redoubles and reinforces our efforts and makes something even better. This is where the old adage "God helps those who help themselves" can be tested and found to be true.

August 16

The courage to create is the courage to make some-thing out of what we are feeling. Out of the swirl of emotions comes some cogent form of expression. It may be a daub of paint. It may be a poem. It may be a few measures of music. Whatever it is, it is the distillate of our human personality. We seek to express what it is that wants to be expressed through us.

August 17

Exercise teaches the rewards of process. It teaches the sense of satisfaction over small tasks well done. Exercise is often the going that moves us from stagnation to inspiration, from problem to solution, from self-pity to self-respect. We *do* learn by going. We learn we are stronger than we thought. We learn to look at things with a new perspective. We learn to solve our problems by tapping our own inner resources and listening for inspiration, not only from others but from ourselves. Seemingly without effort, our answers come while we swim or stride or ride or run. By definition, this is one of the fruits of exercise: "*exercise:* the act of bringing into play or realizing in action" (*Webster's Ninth*).

August 18

The act of making art requires sensitivity, and when we cultivate sufficient sensitivity for our art, we often find that the tumult of life takes a very high toll on our psyches. We become overwrought and overtired. Our energies are drained not by coping with our output of creative energy but from coping with the ceaseless inflow of distractions and distresses that bid for our time, attention, and emotional involvement. As artists, we are great listeners, and as the volume is pitched too high, our inner ear and our inner work suffers. Our inflow level must be kept manageable and we must "train" our friends and families and colleagues at work when and how we need our space, both physical and psychic. This may mean no calls in the morning before eleven. Or voice-mail calls returned every day after three. It may mean "Patience. No contact on demand."

August 19

Allowing art to move through us without impediment means resigning as its author. The work must be allowed to author itself, to take on the shapes and colors that it prefers. I can plan a sequence, but then I must surrender to how the sequence plans itself. This is what we mean by inspiration, the willingness to surrender to a higher octave, the finer vibration that the work itself might hold. Art requires that we relinquish control. It asks us to move out on faith. In this regard, art itself is always one step ahead of the artist, calling us forward.

August 20

Very often, a creative block manifests itself as an addiction to fantasy. Rather than working or living the now, we spin our wheels and indulge in daydreams of could have, would have, should have. One of the great misconceptions about the artistic life is that it entails great swathes of aimlessness. The truth is that a creative life involves great swathes of attention. Attention is a way to connect and survive.

August 21

As an artist, it does me good to have the safety of the Morning Pages that I write daily. There is a steadiness to the Pages. They "mother" me. It also does me good to take an Artist Date, a small soupçon of adventure, a tiny act of daring, like piloting a pony or balancing on the stump of a tree. I do not need a big adventure, just the smallest something will do. When I manage it, I feel my heart tug upward, making its own tricornered smile.

August 22

Creative energy is energy. When we are worrying *about* creating instead of actually creating, we are wasting our creative energy. When we are vacillating, we are letting air out of our tires. Our pickup is not speeding down the road and may never even get out of the driveway. Our project goes flat. Does this mean we should race off wildly? No, but it does mean that once we have a heart's desire we should act on it. It is that action, that moving out on faith, that moves mountains—and careers.

August 23

Blocking is essentially an issue of faith. Rather than trust our intuition, our talent, our skill, our desire, we fear where our creator is taking us with this creativity. Rather than paint, write, dance, audition, and see where it takes us, we pick up a block. Blocked, we know who and what we are: unhappy people. Unblocked, we may be something much more threatening—happy. For most of us, happy is terrifying, unfamiliar, out of control, too risky! Is it any wonder we take temporary U-turns? It takes grace and courage to admit and surrender our blocking devices. Who wants to? Not while they are still working! As we become aware of our blocking devices— food, busyness, alcohol, sex, other drugs—we can feel our U-turns as we make them. The blocks will no longer work effectively. Over time we will try to ride out the anxiety and see where we emerge. Anxiety is fuel. We can use it to write with, paint with, work with.

August 24

"Creations are like children. They pout and sulk," a famous writer recently told me. "If we neglect them they grow petulant. They want our attention." Giving attention to our creations means learning to sense when it is that they need inflow and when it is that they need calm. When our lives become too frantic, our art retreats. It does not thrive on a life lived pell-mell.

August 25

Sometimes as artists, we practice a self-rejecting aesthetic that is like what adolescents do in terms of their physicality. This is the self-loathing that sets in and says whatever we are, it is not as good or as beautiful as whatever it is the other one has. In other words, whatever we are is not what we wish ourselves to be. Comedians yearn for drama; dramatic actors crave comedy. Born short-story writers lust for the National Book Award for their novels; natural novelists scream for the stage. Not that we can't do more than one thing, but one of the things we should let ourselves do is what comes naturally and easily.

August 26

M any times, success comes through unseen doorways. When conventional routes have been exhausted, success steps forward wearing an eccentric cloak. How many times do breaks come to us through sources as unlikely as "my dentist's cousin"? How often do we find that we are led through a maze of lucky breaks and coincidence? "God has a thousand ways to meet you," a minister friend of mine explains. "Do not look for someone else to give your dream permission to go forward. When you make one person or place the source of your lucky break, you are denying the power of God who can work from many corners." Trust God and look for the leadings.

August 27

Creativity requires activity, and this is not good news to most of us. It makes us responsible, and we tend to hate that. You mean I have to *do* something in order to feel better? Yes. And most of us hate to *do* something when we can obsess about something else instead. One of our favorite things to do—instead of our art—is to contemplate the odds. In a creative career, thinking about the odds is a drink of emotional poison. It robs us of the dignity of art-as-process and puts us at the mercy of imagined powers *out there*. Taking this drink quickly leads to a severe and toxic emotional bender. It leads us to ask, "What's the use?" instead of "What's next?" Take one small daily action instead of indulging in the big questions. When we allow ourselves to wallow in the big questions, we fail to find the small answers. What we are talking about here is a concept of change grounded in respect—respect for where we are as well as where we wish to go. We are looking not to grand strokes of change, but instead to the act of creatively husbanding all that is in the present: this job, this house, this relationship.

August 28

One of the difficulties with the creative life is that when we have creative breakthroughs, they may look and even be experienced as breakdowns. Our normal, ordinary way of seeing ourselves and the world suddenly goes on tilt, and as it does, a new way of seeing and looking at things comes toward us. Sometimes this "new vision" can seem almost hallucinogenic in its persuasive shifting of perspective. It is as though we have had a strobe light sweep across our experience and freeze into bas relief a certain previously unquestioned assumption. The creative journey is characterized not by a muzzy and hazy retreat from reality but by the continual sorting and reordering and structuring of reality into new forms and new relationships. As artists, we "see things differently." In part, this is because we are looking.

August 29

Humans are by nature adventurous. Watch a toddler expand his territory a wobbly step at a time. Watch a teenager test curfew. Watch an eighty-year-old grandmother sign up for an art tour of Russia. The soul thrives on adventure. Deprived of adventure, our optimism fails us. Adventure is a nutrient, not a frivolity. When we ignore our need for adventure, we ignore our very nature. Often we do exactly that, calling it "adulthood" or "discipline." When we are too adult and too disciplined, our impish, childlike innovator yearns to rebel.

August 30

When we "forget ourselves," it is easy to write. We are not standing there, stiff as a soldier, our entire ego shimmed into every capital "I." When we forget ourselves, when we let go of being good and settle into just being a writer, we begin to have the experience of writing through us. We retire as the self-conscious author and become something else—the vehicle for self-expression. When we are just the vehicle, the storyteller and not the point of the story, we often write very well—we certainly write more easily.

August 31

It is one of the ironies of the writing life that much of what we write in passing, casually, later seems to hold up just as well as the pieces we slaved over, convinced of their worth and dignity. Ease and difficulty of writing have little to do, in the long run, with the quality of what gets produced. A "bad" writing day can produce good writing. A "good" writing day can produce something we later feel needs a substantial rewrite to make the grade. The point is to value all of what we write, to learn not to be swayed by the mood of the moment into hasty judgments. Too many times, torn-up pages are merely a reflection of our mood and not a reflection of merit.

SEPTEMBER

September 1

Writers procrastinate because they do not feel inspired. Feeling inspired is a luxury. Writing, often excellent writing, can be done without the benefit of feeling inspired. Writers tell themselves they just don't have enough ideas yet, and when they do, then they'll start writing. It actually works exactly backward. When we start to write, we prime the pump and the flow of ideas begins to move. It is the act of writing that calls ideas forward, not ideas that call forward writing.

September 2

Teaching those around us what our priorities are—and remembering them ourselves—makes for harmonious relationships. Clarifying ourselves to others brings honest connections that are grounded in mutual respect. Honesty starts with us. Identifying those who habitually abuse our time and energies is pivotal, but identifying them is only step one. Avoiding them is step two, and this is where a lot of us stumble. It is as if we doubt we have a right to tranquility, respect, and good humor. Shouldn't we really suffer? Shouldn't we find it more spiritual not to upset the status quo? Artificial acceptance of people and circumstances we resent makes us ill tempered. A little honest self-love does wonders for our personality, and for our art.

September 3

Writing can be done by listening to how we feel rather than thinking about how we feel. Writing from the gut is largely a matter of evading the censor. For most of us the censor changes size on a daily basis. Some days the censor is huge, omnivorous, hard to get around; other days, the censor is smaller, a grating little voice of disapproval. The trick is to both miniaturize the censor and to accept the censor—and to write despite what the censor has to say.

September 4

All creative acts require daring, and daring is something that can be learned. We dare, first of all, to accept ourselves as we are in the moment. We dare, next, to accept that that may be enough. Writing from where we are, painting from where we are, acting from where we are, we make beauty of the places we have been. By insisting to ourselves that beauty is present even on those days when we cannot see it, we make the beauty in the world more real. If I felt I were beautiful enough, good enough, and worthy enough, how would I act? Act that way.

September 5

Most blocked creatives carry unacknowledged either/or reasoning that stands between them and their work. To become unblocked we must recognize our either/or thinking. "I can either be romantically happy *or* an artist." It is possible, quite possible, to be both an artist and romantically fulfilled. It is quite possible to be an artist and financially successful.

September 6

There must be some obscure law of physics that revs into action when artists finish something. And that something can be reorganizing the medicine cabinet, cleaning out the glove compartment, or taping your cherished road maps back into usable companions. The moment we finish something, we get a sort of celestial pat—sometimes even a shove—a small booster rocket of energy to be applied elsewhere.

September 7

Anger is fuel. We feel it and we want to do something. Hit someone, break something, throw a fit, smash a fist into the wall, tell those bastards. Be we are *nice* people, and what we do with our anger is stuff it, deny it, bury it, block it, hide it, lie about it, medicate it, muffle it, ignore it. We do everything but *listen* to it. Anger is meant to be listened to. Anger is a voice, a shout, a plea, a demand. Anger is meant to be respected. Why? Because anger is a *map*. Anger shows us what our boundaries are. Anger shows us where we want to go. It lets us see where we've been and lets us know when we haven't liked it. Anger points the way, not just the finger. In the recovery of a blocked artist, anger is a sign of health.

September 8

No surprise that it was Picasso himself who remarked, "We are all born children. The trick is how to remain one." Mozart, we are told, remained one. Why do we get so damn adult? If we stop trying to improve ourselves and start trying to delight ourselves, we get further as artists. If we lean into what we love instead of soldiering toward what we "should," our pace quickens, our energy rises, optimism sets in. What we love is nutritious for us. To be an artist you must learn to let yourself be. Stop getting better. Start appreciating what you are. Do something that simply delights you for no apparent reason. Give in to the little temptation, poke into a strange doorway, buy the weird scrap of silk in a color you never wear. Drop the rock. A lot of great artists work in their pajamas. Ernest Hemingway and Oscar Hammerstein both worked standing up because they liked that.

September 9

We are all artists—some of us are declared, accomplished, and publicly esteemed artists. Others of us are the private kind, making artful homes and artful lives and shying away from the public practice or pursuit of our art. Some of us—officially "not artists" and "without a creative bone in our body"—are artists nonetheless because creativity is in our blood. In our DNA. There is one and only one label that seems useful to me in discussing ourselves. That label is "creative." I have been teaching for over thirty years. (And making art for longer than that.) I have never, *ever* encountered a person who was not creative in some form. Most often, people are creative in many forms. It is the excess of creative energy, not the lack of it, that is what makes people feel—and get labeled—"crazy."

September 10

Creativity is an experience—to my eye, a spiritual experience. It does not matter which way you think of it: creativity leading to spirituality or spirituality leading to creativity. In fact, I do not make a distinction between the two. In the face of such experience, the whole question of belief is rendered obsolete. As Carl Jung answered the question of belief late in his life, "I don't believe; I know."

September 11

The creative imagination is a will-o'-the-wisp. Wooed best by enticement and not by aggressive assault, the imagination responds to being coaxed and cajoled. Just as in romance, too serious, too fast, and the fun fizzles out. We need to flirt with an interest, approach it with a sidelong glance. Children's books might be a better first date with a new interest than enrolling in a master's program. More is very nice as something to look forward to and not so nice as part of the phrase "More than I could handle or absorb." Adventures should be manageable, not overwhelming. It is one of the paradoxes of the sustained creative life that the more lightly we take ourselves, the more serious work we will probably be able to do. The more we bear down on ourselves, the more constricted we will feel, and the more vulnerable we will be to creative injury.

September 12

As our success and visibility as artists rise, so does the flow of two often difficult to distinguish things: opportunities and diversions. It is no coincidence that in Chinese the hexagram for "opportunity" and "crisis" are the same. As we become brighter and stronger as artists, others are attracted by that clarity and glow. Some of them will help us on our way, while others will try to help themselves, diverting our creative light to their own path. Those who actually offer us invitations and work in alignment with our true values and goals are opportunities to be cherished, and colleagues to bond with. Those who covertly present their own agendas in the disguise of a lucky break for us are opportunists, not opportunities. They represent a creative crisis in the making. They are what I call "piggybackers," and they must be identified and weeded out of our creative garden.

September 13

Using our creativity is therapeutic, but not because we need to be fixed. What we need is to be expressive. What's inside us is not all nasty and horrid and terrifying, not all shame and secrets and neurosis. Our inner world is a complex, exquisite, and powerful play of colors, lights, and shadows, a cathedral of consciousness as glorious as the natural world itself. This inner wealth is what the artist expresses. The Great Creator lives within each of us. All of us contain a divine, expressive spark, a creative candle intended to light our path and that of our fellows. We are shiny, not tarnished; large, not small; beautiful, not damaged—although we may be ignorant of our grace, power, and dignity.

September 14

When writing is perceived as channeling spiritual information rather than inventing intellectual information, writing becomes a more fluid process that we are no longer charged with self-consciously guarding. Instead, we are charged with being available to it. We can "plug in" to the flow of writing rather than thinking of it as a stream of energy we must generate from within ourself.

September 15

A creative person is intended to be fed and supported by both divine and human sources, but none of those needed nutrients can reach us if we have turned ourselves into a food source for others, allowing them to dine freely on our time, our talents and our reserves. Creativity expands in an atmosphere encouraging to it, and constricts self-protectively in an atmosphere that is cynical or hostile. This is why our close friends must be safe and smart, but not so smart-aleck that our creative child is afraid to speak up. When we lose our voice or our energy creatively, it is not some mysterious malady. It can usually be traced directly to an encounter in which our energy was abused.

September 16

While our mythology tells us that writing is about the ivory tower, writing itself teaches an interest in life outside the tower. The artist is not a prisoner of art locked in the prison of the self. No! Art sets the artist free. Art is the key to freedom. Art is the doorway to a larger, livelier, and more involved self. I have said "an involved self" and not "self-involved." The consistent practice of art is a bridge between the self and the world.

September 17

For artists, few things feel better than a sense of propulsion. The feeling of forward motion in our art brings us a deep and abiding happiness, carrying with it feelings of self-esteem. When we are procrastinating—"waiting for it to become easier"—we inevitably feel bad about ourselves. Nothing takes the place of actually doing the work, of being able to say at day's end, "I accomplished that."

September 18

We must recognize that God is unlimited in supply and that everyone has equal access. This begins to clear up guilt about having or getting too much. Since everyone can draw on the universal supply, we deprive no one with our abundance. If we learn to think of receiving God's good as being an act of worship—cooperating with God's plan to manifest goodness in our lives—we can begin to let go of having to sabotage ourselves.

September 19

When we "reach" for a word in our writing, we need to reach inward, not outward. The body has the word for us if we will just listen to what it volunteers. Touch is incredibly precise, delicate, and powerful; we say we want our writing to "touch" people, but we seldom look at the fact that in order to do so it must embody our actual experience. Our language must be physical. This is how we "touch" our reader.

September 20

Worry is the imagination's negative stepsister. Instead of making things, we make trouble. Culturally, we are trained to worry. When we focus our imaginations to inhabit the positive, the same creative energy that was worry can become something else. I have written poems, songs, entire plays with "anxiety." When worry strikes, remind yourself your gift for worry and negativity is merely a sure sign of your considerable creative powers. It is the proof of the creative potential you have for making your life better, not worse.

September 21

Very often in our creative lives we can feel ourselves in jeopardy. We may have a sudden and debilitating doubt that our work will continue to be supported by the Universe. We may have been earning a living so far, but that's so far—our fear says—and so far is no guarantee of tomorrow. Rather than trust that there is an unseen but benevolent web gently holding us in our place, we often panic and act like we have gotten where we have gotten entirely on our own. But there is a benevolent web that holds us gently in our place. There *is* a larger power that wishes us well. We are led well and carefully. In order to be led further, we need only to ask for help. Help is always available to us. We need to open ourselves up. We need to be receptive.

September 22

Our creative energy is our divine inheritance. If people insist on squandering it and we cooperate, we will find ourselves creatively bankrupt, drained of goodwill and good feelings, short-tempered and short-fused. As artists, we must husband our energy as carefully as our money. We must spend it along lines that are personally and creatively rewarding. We must invest it wisely in people and projects that return our investment with measurable satisfaction, growth, and achievement.

September 23

All artists get discouraged. All artists have deep inner wells of self-pity into which we periodically dive. All artists are doing better than someone else and worse than someone else. All artists are doing better today than they have in the past and worse than they will in the future. All artists specialize in self-doubt. It is how we hone the creative imagination.

September 24

Your artist is a child. Find and protect that child. Learning to let yourself create is like learning to walk. The artist child must begin by crawling. Baby steps will follow and there will be falls—horrible first paintings, beginning films that look like unedited home movies, first poems that would shame a greeting card. Typically, the recovering shadow artist will use these early efforts to discourage continued exploration. Judging your early artistic efforts is artist abuse.

September 25

Most of us think we can't write. We think it's something other people do—"writers." Or, if you have a novice's happy skill and amateur's fervent love, it's a name you reserve for the skill belonging to "real writers." If we eliminate the word "writer," if we just go back to writing as an act of listening and naming what we hear, some of the rules disappear. There is an organic shape, a form-coming-into-form that is inherent in the thing we are observing. Shape does not need to be imposed. When we just let ourselves write, we get it "right."

September 26

There is a connection between self-nurturing and self-respect. If I allow myself to be bullied and cowed by other people's urges for me to be more normal or more nice, I sell myself out. They may like me better, feel more comfortable with my more conventional appearance or behavior, but I will hate myself. Hating myself, I may lash out at myself and others.

September 27

It is difficult when we are constricted by fear to allow ourselves the expansion of an Artist Date, and yet this is the very medicine we need. On an Artist Date we sense that we are part of a larger world. In this larger world, our dreams and ambitions have their place.

September 28

What writing brings to a life is clarity and tenderness. Writing, we witness ourselves. We say, like our own village elders, "I knew you when you were knee high and you've certainly come a long way." Writing gives us a place to say what we need to say, but also to hear what we need to hear.

September 29

When we are incubating something creatively, we follow a cycle of seasons. We begin locked in winter, when we look and feel devoid of ideas, although the ideas are there for us, simply dormant. Our wintry hearts lurch toward spring and suddenly an idea puts out a hopeful bud. The idea may be as festive as the buoyant pink cherry blossoms. Our idea is bright and indisputable. We blossom as the landscape does. And then what happens? As surely as the seasons turn, our brightly budded ideas must now ripen and mature. Spring turns the corner into summer. Showy pink gives way to industrious green. Now come the long days of labor. We must work to bring forth the fruit of what we have envisioned.

September 30

The artist is a cartographer; he maps the world. The world within him, and the world as he sees it. Sometimes that world is very strange. A great work of art focuses the imagination of a vast audience on a previously inchoate problem. *The Grapes of Wrath* showed us the Depression. *One Flew Over the Cuckoo's Nest* showed us our democratic horror at institutions run amuck. All novels are "novel" because they are seeking to tell us something new. Known or unknown, famous or anonymous, all art is an attempt to map the territory of the heart.

OCTOBER

October 1

Practice means what it says: writing is something to be done over and over, something that improves through the repetitive doing but that needs not be done perfectly. Just as a piano teacher will tell you to practice scales, that consistency is the key to mastering the instrument, as a writing teacher I have said the same thing. Consistency is the key to mastering the instrument that is you.

October 2

It is all too easy as an artist to allow the shape of our career to be dictated to us by others. We can so easily wait to be chosen. Such passivity invites despair. To remain healthy and vital, artists must stay proactive in their own behalf. Writers must write for the love of writing and not merely, or only, to fulfill a book contract. Actors must consciously choose ways to keep acting when they are not winning auditions. As an artist, I must be alert to keeping myself in effective training. Like a creative triathlete, I must take care to be well-rounded. I must take stock of my talents and take the time and care to try to use them fully.

October 3

Dependence on the creator within is really freedom from all other dependencies. Paradoxically, it is also the only route to real intimacy with other human beings. Freed from our terrible fears of abandonment, we are able to live with more spontaneity. Freed from our constant demands for more and more reassurance, our fellows are able to love us back without feeling so burdened. As we come to trust and love our internal guide, we lose our fear of intimacy because we no longer confuse our intimate others with the higher power we are coming to know. We place our dependency on the source itself. The source meets our needs through people, places, and things.

October 4

Most writers don't want to hear that there are some very straightforward cures for procrastination. A daily habit of Morning Pages will train the censor to stand aside and make procrastination much more difficult to practice on any and all writing. Artist Dates will create an inner welling up of thoughts and ideas that will become more and more pressing to put on the page. Blasting Through Blocks, a quick listing of fears and resentments about a project, will often swiftly clear the channel to write. Above all else, a week of Media Deprivation in which you do not read, watch TV, see movies, or listen to talk radio will force even the most adroit procrastinator toward the page with a certain eagerness.

October 5

Writing is a way not only to metabolize life but to transform what happens to us into our own experience. It is a way to move from passive to active. We may still be the victims of circumstance, but by our understanding those circumstances we place events within the ongoing context of our own life, that is, the life we "own."

October 6

As you learn to recognize, nurture, and protect your inner artist, you will be able to move beyond pain and creative constriction. You will learn ways to recognize and resolve fear, remove emotional scar tissue, and strengthen your confidence. Damaging old ideas about creativity will be explored and discarded. You will experience an intensive encounter with your own creativity—your private villains, champions, wishes, fears, dreams, hopes, and triumphs. The experience will make you excited, depressed, angry, afraid, joyous, hopeful, and, ultimately, more free.

October 7

When we are focused on the possible, we are able to ignore the probable. We are able to set aside that tricky question of odds. The odds stacked against us as an artist immediately lessen if we are in fact doing our work. The odds of publishing a novel are a hell of a lot higher if you have written a novel. In other words, when we can focus on what it is we are doing, then what it is we could do becomes a logical progression and not a wild fantasy.

October 8

Once we accept that creativity is a spiritual act, it doesn't seem like a far jump to expect such synchronicity to be at hand. There is a benevolent Something that is kindly toward ourselves and our art. The Great Creator is an artist and loves other artists. The Divine does play a hand in what it is we are making. We can consciously choose to invite divine participation. We can ask for and receive divine help and guidance. We do not need to feel that our dreams and God's will for us are at opposite ends of the table. We can consider the possibility that our dreams come from God and that God has a plan for their proper unfolding. When we seek daily spiritual guidance, we are guided toward the next step forward for our art. It will come to us as the hunch, the inkling, the itch. It will come to us as timely conversations with others. It will come to us in many ways—but it will come to us.

October 9

Fame is a spiritual drug. It is often a by-product of our artistic work, but like nuclear waste, it can be a very dangerous by-product. Fame, the desire to attain it, the desire to hold on to it, can produce the "How am I doing?" syndrome. This question is not "Is the work going well?" This question is "How does it look to them?" The point of the work *is* the work. Fame interferes with that perception. Fame is really a shortcut for self-approval. Try approving of yourself just as you are. Treating yourself like a precious object will make you strong. What's in order here is a great deal of gentleness and some behavior that makes you like yourself. What we are really scared of is that without fame we won't be loved—as artists or as people. The solution to this fear is concrete, small, loving actions. We must actively, consciously, consistently, and creatively nurture our artist selves.

October 10

Competition is another spiritual drug, and lies at the root of much creative blockage. When we focus on competition we poison our own well, impede our own progress. When we are ogling the accomplishments of others, we take our eye away from our own through line. We ask ourselves the wrong questions, and those wrong questions give us the wrong answers. As artists, we must go within. We must attend to what it is our inner guidance is nudging us toward. As artists, we cannot afford to think about who is getting ahead of us and how they don't deserve it. The desire to *be better than* can choke off the simple desire to *be*. As artists we cannot afford this thinking.

October 11

The reward for attention is always healing. It may begin as the healing of a particular pain—the lost lover, the sickly child, the shattered dream. But what is healed, finally, is the pain that underlies all pain: the pain that we are all, as Rilke phrases it, "unutterably alone." More than anything else, attention is an act of connection.

October 12

A critical failure of nerve at the last moment causes us to doubt the worthiness of projects we have birthed. Novels go into desk drawers. Plays languish on shelves. The pumpkin rots on the vine. How can we go forward from here? We must believe, first of all, in the worth of our brainchildren. We must not abandon them. We must keep them a priority. Faced with rejection, we must keep trying. At root, it comes back to being a matter of faith. We must see our work as divine in origin. We must believe there is a divine path of goodness ahead in its unfolding. When we are rejected, we must ask, "What next?" and not, "Why me?"

October 13

The ego hates to rest. The ego doesn't want to let God, or sleep, mend up the raveled sleeve of care. The ego would like to handle all that itself, thank you. As artists, we must serve our souls, not our egos. Our souls need rest. So often we try to gird ourselves to face a harsh and difficult world when we might instead gentle both ourselves and our world just by slowing down. Even God rested. Even waves rest. Even business titans close their office doors and play with the secret toys on their desks. Our language of creativity knows this. We talk about "the play of ideas," but we still overwork and underplay and wonder why we feel so drained.

October 14

I am not sure where we got the idea that in order to be "real" artists we had to do things perfectly. The minute we see the word "perfect" (and I think critics are the ones who drag it in the door), spontaneity goes out the window. We get so sure that we can't be a great composer that we never let ourselves write our kids a goofy lullaby or play improvisational noodles at the piano. We're so respectful of "great" art that we always, chronically, sell ourselves short. Here's what I like about God: Trees are crooked, mountains are lumpy, a lot of his creatures are funny-looking, and he made it all anyway. He didn't let the aardvark convince him he had no business designing creatures. He didn't make a puffer fish and get discouraged. No, the maker made things—and still does.

October 15

Anger is a call to action. Anger asks us to step up to the plate for ourselves and for others. It points to a path we are trying to avoid. Anger signals us that we are being called to step forward and speak out. Anger is a profoundly powerful fuel that we can use to make art and to make more artful lives. When we deny our anger or fritter it away in complaints, we are wasting precious fuel and precious clarity. Anger is a searchlight. It shows us our moral terrain and it shows us the damage we feel done to that terrain by others. It shows us, above all, our choices. Anger causes poems, plays, novels, films. Anger causes symphonies and paintings. When we think of our anger as something that should be excised or denied rather than alchemized, we risk neutering ourselves as artists.

October 16

It can be said that our talents are gifts from God and our use of our talents is our gift back to God. The degree of happiness we experience when working well, the sense of rightness and harmony, all argue that creativity is God's will for us. When we create, we work hand in glove with the Great Creator. Creativity is its nature and our own. We think—and manifest—from the mind of God within us.

October 17

At root, self-pity is a stalling device. It is a temper tantrum, a self-inflicted drama that has little to do, ever, with the facts. Self-pity isn't very interested in facts. What it likes is "stories." Self-pity thrives on stories that go, "Poor innocent me and terrible, mean them . . ." Self-pity likes to make us feel the world is an adversarial place and that the odds are stacked against us. Self-pity likes to point out the way we are never truly appreciated, valued, cherished. What self-pity really wants is a cheering section and a fan club. Although self-pity *appears* to be grounded in the lack of appreciation from others, it is *actually* grounded in our *own* discounting of our self and our struggles. A few tears of sorrow over work ill used, a moment of surrender to our genuine fatigue and heartbreak—a little actual grief can very quickly take the claws out of self-pity's hold on us. When we say, "Of course you feel bad," then we are on the brink of something a little interesting. We begin to raise the question "If this makes me feel so bad, what can I change?" and that question snaps us back onto our own creative spine.

October 18

Art opens the closets, airs out the cellars and attics. It brings healing. But before a wound can heal it must be seen, and this act of exposing the wound to air and light, the artist's act, is often reacted to with shaming. Bad reviews are a prime source of shame for many artists. The truth is, many reviews do aim at creating shame in an artist. "Shame on you! How dare you make that rotten piece of art?" When people do not want to see something, they get mad at the one who shows them. They kill the messenger.

October 19

As artists, we must cultivate faith. We must learn to see beyond appearances. We must trust that there is something larger and more benevolent than the apparent odds stacked against us. For the sake of sheer survival, we artists must learn to have a deep and abiding belief in our own work and its worthiness, despite the world's apparent acceptance or rejection. As artists, we have a vocation. There is Something that "calls" to us to work. In answering that call and making art, we keep our side of the bargain. Our efforts will be rewarded, although not perhaps in the ways that we had planned.

October 20

As artists, we must be resilient. Delicate as we are, we must also be stalwart. We must take our cue from the natural world and vow to be like the perennial flowers, stubbornly reappearing season after season. There is some simple dignity that lies in the labor of doing the art for art's sake and not for the glory and acclaim that we hope to accrue. We are creations and we are intended, in turn, to be creative ourselves. Like the flowers, we are intended to blossom. We must make art for the sheer sake of making art. That is being true to our nature. That is being true to our path.

October 21

I think we have to admit that we do not own our art. It owns us. I think the sooner we admit that and try to relinquish control, the better off we are. For some reason, God has chosen some of us to write and we have little to do with it. I believe all people are creative, and that I have been given this form as my own. I have to try to set my ego aside and stop letting it vote on everything that I do. The ego's votes are so often incorrect. If only I could remember that.

October 22

We are intended to be conduits for inspiration. There are high thoughts and high intentions and higher realms that can speak to us and through us if we allow it. When our ego and our ego-driven fears are given a central place as regards our art, we have rolled a large boulder into our own way, and our career cannot unfold unimpeded because it must divide to make its way with unnatural intensity and velocity around the boulder settled in the stream of our good. On rivers and in the rivers of creative flow, such rapids are treacherous. We are far better served by being of service.

October 23

So much of an artist's career hinges on the sense that we are going somewhere, that we are not just trapped by the four walls of wherever we are. For creative sanity, I must believe that if I just do the next right thing, a path will unfold for me. I must believe there is a divine plan for me and my work. As an artist, I must believe in higher forces, sources of inspiration, movements of destiny. I must believe in something larger and wiser than myself. Some artists believe in God. Others believe in Art. No matter what we call it, a belief in it is necessary for our sheer artistic survival.

October 24

We have to free ourselves from determining our value and the value of our work by that work's market value. The idea that money validates credibility is very hard to shake. If money determines real art, then Gauguin was a charlatan. We must learn that as artists our credibility lies with us, with God, and with our work. In other words, if you have a poem to write, you need to write that poem—whether it will sell or not.

October 25

For over three decades, I have been working with students and watching those students transform their lives through writing. I have seen shy and timorous students claim their right. I have seen bombastic, blow-hard students gently deflate their own egos and become user-friendly members of the human tribe. I have watched people open themselves to deeper relationships, extricate themselves from difficult relationships, change jobs, and change identities. I have seen writing work less like a tool than a medicine. It is a medicine all of us can make and administer to ourselves.

October 26

Two variables seem essential for life to feel benefi-cent. One variable is stability. The other is change. Writing supplies a sense of both variables. Writing both gives continuity and creates a sense of continuity. Writing both gives change and creates an awareness of change. A writing life is therefore—far from what our mythology around writing tells us—very often a life with substantial happiness at its core. Writing to find happiness, I find my happiness—writing.

October 27

I want us to take back the power into our own hands. I want us to remember we have choices and voices. I want us to right our world, and writing is the tool I feel helps us to do it. We are a restless lot here in the West. We do not take easily to meditation. Writing is an active form of meditation that lets us examine our lives and see where and how we can alter them to make them more sound. Yes, writing is an art, but "art" is part of the verb "to be"—as in "Thou art truly human." To be truly human, we all have the right to make art. We all have the right to write.

October 28

There is one and only one cure for a creative injury, and that cure is to make something. If we do not make some small something, our injured yet active imagination will make an even bigger deal out of what happened to us. Sometimes, the only comfort we can find is naming ourselves. If no one else will pronounce us "artist," then we must say our name to ourselves—and the only way to say it is through art. The bandage must fit the wound.

October 29

"God is in the details," exclaimed Ludwig Mies van der Rohe. Writing specifically, writing detail by detail, we encounter not only ourselves, not only our truth, but the greater truth that stands behind all art and all communication. We touch the spiritual fact that as divided as we may feel ourselves to be, we are nonetheless One. That is the central fact that all real writing communicates—and it does it specifically.

October 30

As an artist, I do best when reaching for humility. I must be willing to be just a worker among workers, just an artist among artists. Competition has no place in this scenario. Competition creates stress. Stress creates constriction and constriction creates block. Think of your artist as an emotional youngster. For that youngster, it's scary to be the center of attention. The glare of the spotlight can create the paralysis of block. To function freely as an artist, I must take the focus off of winning, off of being the brightest and the best. I must give up such ego-driven notions as being "fascinating" and "brilliant." I need a safe, critic-free arena in which to do my work. Then, with the ground rules in place, I must gently go forward.

October 31

If you'll pardon the levity, most of us are afraid of fear. We think it's a bad thing. We *know* it's a scary thing. We're afraid of becoming afraid, scared of becoming scared. We know all too well how our fears can escalate into terror, and how our terror can either translate into frantic action or into paralyzing inertia. Because so many of our experiences with fear have been negative, we fail to see fear as positive or useful. It is both. Let me repeat: Fear is positive and useful. Fear is a blip on the radar screen of our consciousness. It is something we catch out of the corner of our eye. Fear tells us "Check this out." It enters our thoughts the way a dark shadow looks across a doorway. "Is someone there?" we may gasp. Yes, someone is there. Often it is a perception spoken by a part of ourselves that we have neglected and failed to attend. Fear asks that we check something for clarity. Fear requires action, not assurance.

NOVEMBER

November 1

It is one of the most frequent fears among would-be writers that they are simply "not original enough." They forget that the root word in "original" is "origin." We are the origin of our work. If that origin is mapped accurately enough, if we are honest enough to name what we find there, then our work is original.

November 2

Many of us find that we have squandered our own creative energies by investing disproportionately in the lives, hopes, dreams, and plans of others. Their lives have obscured and detoured our own. As we consolidate a core through our withdrawal process, we become more able to articulate our own boundaries, dreams, and authentic goals. Our personal flexibility increases while our malleability to the whims of others decreases. We experience a heightened sense of autonomy and possibility.

November 3

In centuries past, art was made for the honor and glory of God. Viewed in this light, a career in the arts was a career of service, not egotism. There is a cue there for us. The dedication of our work to a higher cause than our own self-promotion frees the work from preciousness. It becomes not about how good we are but about how good we can be in selfless service to something larger than ourselves. As artists, we are the bearers of gifts, spiritual endowments that come to us gratis and ask only to be used. A gift for music asks that we give voice to it. A fine photographer's eye asks that we focus it. We are responsible to our gifts for the use of our gifts, and this is a form of accountability too.

November 4

It is my belief that any regular practice is a good practice. It is my belief that if you bicycle, it will teach you. If you walk, it will teach you. If you bake bread or write poems, it will teach you. What will teach you is the "it" that you do because that "it" is doing you: doing you a favor, doing you a service, doing you a good turn, a grace, a job.

November 5

Workaholism is an addiction, and like all addictions, it blocks creative energy. In fact, it could be argued that the desire to block the fierce flow of creative energy is an underlying reason for addiction. If people are too busy to write Morning Pages, or too busy to take an Artist Date, they are probably too busy to hear the voice of authentic creative urges. Only recently recognized as an addiction, workaholism still receives a great deal of support in our society. The phrase *I'm working* has a certain unassailable air of goodness and duty to it. The truth is, we are very often working to avoid ourselves, our spouses, our real feelings. In creative recovery, it is far easier to get people to do the extra work of the Morning Pages than it is to get them to do the assigned play of an Artist Date. Play can make a workaholic very nervous. Fun is scary.

November 6

Life is made of small sweetnesses, and they come to us when we are willing to be little, instead of big. What do I mean by being willing to be little? I mean that on a gray day we count the beauty of the raindrops hanging from the fire escape railing. We listen for the song of birds even though those birds are out of sight. A gray day is a good day to polish a pair of shoes, to put new laces in your sneakers, to run a damp cloth along the window ledges cleaning up the grime. On a gray day, we are like children and perhaps it is a good day to act like them.

November 7

In our personal friendships, we require peers who see and acknowledge the skills we bring to the table. It is perfectly fine to talk with friends about our career situations and our fiscal dilemmas, but if those friends are giving us advice from their own considerable professional acuity and attainment, that should get some small nod from us, as ours hopefully does from them. This reciprocity of respect may be largely tacit, but it must be there. We deserve recognition and respect and acknowledgment for the actual worth of our investments of time, talent, and keen observation.

November 8

It is important to be able to sort useful criticism from the other kind. Often we need to do the sorting out for ourselves, without the benefit of a public vindication. As artists, we are far more able to do this sorting than people might suspect. Pointed criticism, if accurate, often gives the artist an inner sense of relief. Useful criticism ultimately leaves us with one more puzzle piece for our work. Useless criticism, on the other hand, leaves us with a feeling of being bludgeoned. As a rule, it is withering and shaming in tone; ambiguous in content; personal, inaccurate, or blanket in its condemnations. There is nothing to be gleaned from irresponsible criticism. You are dealing with an inner child. Artistic child abuse creates rebellion creates block. All that can be done with abusive criticism is to heal from it.

November 9

Have you considered asking your creative saints, those artists you admire who have passed over, for help? This personal practice, far from being heretical, honors the fact that art making is a spiritual lineage. Our artistic ancestors *are* sources of inspiration, not only in the survival of their work but in the survival of their creative spirit. By involving them directly, we correctly honor their contributions to our lives, and this practice often yields great creative fruit.

November 10

We hear so often that the artist's temperament is restless, irritable, and discontented. All of that is very true—when we are not working. Let us get in a good day at the page or the easel and we are suddenly sunny and user-friendly. It is the blocked artist who is such a study in malcontent. Artists have an itch that nothing can scratch except work.

November 11

*B*e *very careful to safeguard your newly recovering artist.* Often, creativity is blocked by our falling in with other people's plans for us. We want to set aside time for our creative work, but we feel we *should* do something else instead. As blocked creatives, we focus not on our responsibilities to ourselves, but on our responsibilities to others. We tend to think such behavior makes us good people. It doesn't. It makes us frustrated people. The essential element in nurturing our creativity lies in nurturing ourselves. Through self-nurturance we nurture our inner connection to the Great Creator. Through this connection our creativity will unfold. Paths will appear for us. We need to trust the Great Creator and move out in faith.

November 12

Inner malcontent actually triggers outer change—if we are willing to listen to our malcontent with an open mind and listen to what will feel like a wave of irrational promptings. Those oddball, harebrained, nonlinear, and screwball itches, hunches, and urges are the path through the briar patch. Follow your strange creative cravings and you will be led into change a step at a time.

November 13

It is a spiritual law that when we are ready to transform, transformation will come to us. We are all conduits for a great creative energy that seeks expression in us and through us. When we yearn to be different, it is not just our restless ego. It is our accurate response to the creative energy within us that is seeking a new venue for expression. We are all creative and we are, in turn, creations. Just as we get restless to make something new, so, too, our creator may be restless to make something new from us. As we let go of our ego's demands to be totally in charge, we slip gently and quietly into a series of changes that we may set in motion through our own hand but experience as the hand of the Great Creator working through us. As we do as inwardly directed, a direction emerges. The spiritual shorthand for this is the phrase "Take one step toward God and discover that God has taken a thousand steps toward you."

November 14

So often in a creative career, the magic that is required is quite simply the courage to go on. Singers must sing their scales. Actors must learn their monologues. Writers like myself must spend time at the keys. We would like a break in the weather. We would like a break, period, but the breaks, if they come, will not come today. Today is about keeping on.

November 15

As artists, we are innovators. We experiment and explore. We make things new—at the very least we make things anew. Every painting edges us forward a hair in skill and experience, even if we are in a workshop class that copies an old master. A new staging of an old ballet, the millionth high school production of *Romeo and Juliet*—each expression of art breathes new breath into the work and into the world. Even when we are doing something that "has been done," we bring to bear fresh creative energy. And when we deliberately explore and extend our creative territory, we innovate even further and even more.

November 16

There is always a way to move forward. We may be blinded at times by our own belief in conventions. We may say, "I cannot go forward without a producer," or "I cannot go forward without a director," but the truth is that God is both a producer and a director and often we can move forward if we are willing, one more time, to trust a wing and a prayer.

November 17

As artists, we have antennae sensitive to the thoughts and feelings of those around us. We can be chilled by indifference, hurt by lack of consideration, and we can be exhausted and diminished if we are in the company of those who talk down to us or treat us subtly like the identified patient: "Oh, you and your crazy ideas." As artists, we *need* our crazy ideas, and we need those who don't think they're too crazy. Symphonies and screenplays begin as crazy ideas. So do novels and nocturnes, bronzes and ballets.

November 18

Answered prayers are scary. They imply responsibility. You asked for it. Now that you've got it, what are you going to do? Answered prayers deliver us back to our own hand. This is not comfortable. We find it easier to accept them as examples of synchronicity. It's my experience that we're much more afraid that there might be a God than we are that there might not be. People talk about how dreadful it would be if there were no God. I think such talk is hooey. Most of us are a lot more comfortable feeling we're not being watched too closely.

November 19

As artists, we know very well that something can "not be done," only until someone does it. Some artist, somewhere, decides to shove the fence back a little and extend his or her and all of our range. As artists, we must listen most carefully to our inner guidance and secondarily to our outer advisers. This isn't just spiritual law—trusting the still, small voice to guide us—it's good business practice as well. The interaction of commerce and creativity is a tricky dance, and we as artists must lead it. Show a new direction in your painting to a dealer who is being asked for more of last year's series and you may hear a worried and dispiriting "Mmmm." Do not be fooled. He cannot see what you as an artist may sense, that your direction is the new direction the market will soon be following. For an artist willing to have a learning curve, all directions lead to somewhere worthy.

November 20

An affirmation is a positive statement of (positive) belief, and if we can become one-tenth as good at positive self-talk as we are at negative self-talk, we will notice an enormous change. *Affirmations help achieve a sense of safety and hope.* But saying nice things about ourselves is hard to do. It feels pretty awful at first. Try picking an affirmation. For example "I, _____ (your name), am a brilliant and prolific potter (painter, poet, or whatever you are)." Write that ten times in a row.

November 21

Trusting our creativity is new behavior for many of us. It may feel quite threatening initially, not only to us but also to our intimates. We may feel—and look—erratic. This is a normal part of getting unstuck, pulling free from the muck that has blocked us. It is important to remember that at first flush, going *sane* feels just like going crazy. There is a recognizable ebb and flow to the process of recovering our creative selves. As we gain strength, so will some of the attacks of self-doubt. This is normal, and we can deal with these stronger attacks when we see them as symptoms of recovery.

November 22

The human being, by definition, is a creative being. We are intended to make things and, in the old phrase, to "make something of ourselves." When we lose interest in ourselves and our lives, when we tell ourselves our dreams don't matter or that they are impossible, we are denying our spiritual heritage. When we do this, we become depressed and drained, even physically ill. We become snappish, irritable, high-strung. We call ourselves neurotic—this is not the case. We are not neurotic, we are miserable—miserable because we have stifled our creative selves. Those selves are alive—well—and too large for the cage we have put them in, the cage we call "normal." In our culture we are trained to hide ourselves and punished when we show ourselves. So we hide ourselves from others and from ourselves. It is the hiding of our true nature that makes us feel or act crazy.

November 23

It is my experience both as an artist and as a teacher that when we move out of faith into the act of creation, the universe is able to advance. It is a little like opening the gate at the top of a field irrigation system. Once we remove the blocks, the flow moves in. I do not ask you to *believe* this. In order for this creative emergence to happen, you don't have to believe in God. I simply ask you to observe and note this process as it unfolds. In effect, you will be midwiving and witnessing your own creative progression.

November 24

As artists, most of us contain a highly evolved and sharp-clawed inner perfectionist. This perfectionist has nothing to do with having standards and everything to do with self-punishing, self-flagellating, and self-defeating premature judgments regarding our potential. The root word of "potential" is "potency," or "power." Just as the eagle's fledgling is less formidable than the eventual eagle, so too, our embryonic steps in a new art form fail to accurately convey our later creative flight.

November 25

In times of pain, when the future is too terrifying to contemplate and the past too painful to remember, I have learned to pay attention to right now. The precise moment I was in was always the only safe place for me. Each moment, taken alone, was always bearable. In the exact now, we are all, always, all right. I am breathing in and out. Realizing this, I begin to notice that each moment is not without its beauty.

November 26

I sometimes think of the critic as a character left over from caveman times, times concerned with sheer survival. The critic hunches at the edge of the clearing and watches for dangerous intruders. If we send in an original thought, that thought is often shooed away. To the critic, an original thought may appear disturbing, even dangerous. It wants to see what it has seen before. To the critic, ease feels foreign—and suspicious. Work should be work, shouldn't it? The critic believes in product, not process. It does not like us to have the joy of creation. It is interested in fixing things, not in creating things. It insists there must always be something to fix.

November 27

In striving to clear the way for our creative flow, we must look at our work habits very clearly. We may not think we overwork until we look at the hours we put in. We may think our work is normal until we compare it with a normal forty-hour week. One way to achieve clarity about our time expenditures is to keep a daily checklist and record of our time spent. Even an hour of creative work/play can go a long way toward offsetting the sense of workaholic desperation that keeps our dreams at bay. Because workaholism is a process addiction (an addiction to a behavior rather than a substance), it is difficult to tell when we are indulging in it. An alcoholic gets sober by abstaining from alcohol. A workaholic gets sober by abstaining from *over*work.

November 28

As artists, when human powers fail us, we must turn to the Great Creator for help. We must "surrender" our sense of isolation and despair and open ourselves to the spiritual help we frequently experience as an unexpected inner strength. Let me be clear about one thing: Artists at all levels experience adversity—some of us quite publicly, some of us in painful privacy. One way or another—bad colleagues, bad reviews—we fall off the horse. It is a spiritual law that no loss is without meaning in all of creation. In my experience, an artist's anguished prayers are *always* answered by the Great Creator. Even as we sob to the fates, and rightly, "I cannot go on," we are going on, and we are going on with spiritual assistance. Something is stirring that means we are already going on.

November 29

When faced with a loss, immediately take one small action to support your artist. Even if all you are doing is buying a bunch of tulips and a sketch pad, your action says, "I acknowledge you and your pain. I promise you a future worth having." Like a small child, our artist needs mommying. "Ouch. That hurt. Here's a little treat, a lullaby, a promise."

November 30

So many things are out of our control, but making art *is* in our control. There is always a small and doable creative something we can do if we are willing to move ahead without a guarantee. We may not be able to work at our art on the level that we wish we could, but we can always do something. When we commit ourselves to the process of art and not to the need to produce a saleable product, we begin to experience the joy of creation.

DECEMBER

December 1

Perfectionism doesn't believe in practice shots. It doesn't believe in improvement. Perfectionism has never heard that anything worth doing is worth doing badly—and that if we allow ourselves to do something badly we might in time become quite good at it. Perfection measures our beginner's work against the finished work of masters. Perfectionism thrives on comparison and competition. It doesn't know how to say, "Good try," or "Job well done." The critic does not believe in creative glee—or any glee at all, for that matter. No, perfectionism is a serious matter.

December 2

Yes, youth passes behind us, but we are blind so often to what we are gaining and to the beauty of what we become as artists. There is not a note of silvery sound or a hair turned silver that isn't perfect and beautiful. It is difficult not to rage at the passing of physical beauty and strength, the exquisite daring and dexterity we once possessed, the turn of a phrase or a haunch as perfect as a ripe peach—of course we miss these things. But we gain in beauty. We gain in tenderness. We gain in longing and desire and in satiation if we get the chance—not merely or only exquisitely in our sexual and our physical selves but our creative selves as well.

December 3

It may well be that the "self" in self-expression is not only the voice of our finite, individual self but also the voice of the Self, that larger and higher force of which we are both subject and substance. When we express our creativity, we are a conduit for the Great Creator to explore, express, and expand its divine nature and our own. We are like songbirds. When one of us gives voice to our true nature, it is contagious and others soon give tongue as well. There is an infallibility to the law that as we each seek to express what we are longing to say, there is always someone or something that is longing to hear precisely what we have expressed. We do not live or create in isolation. Each of us is part of a greater whole and, as we agree to express ourselves, we agree to express the larger Self that moves through us all.

December 4

As artists, we must be very careful to protect ourselves and our work from premature questions and assumptions. It is not appropriate to describe our work in a few short sentences, watching the look of interest turn into one of "I'll pass" on the listener's face. Talk uses creative power. Talk dilutes our feelings and passions. Not always, but usually. It is only talk with the right person and at the right time that is useful. Our ideas are valuable. Sharing them with someone who is not discerning is like being talked out of a precious stone—you knew it was a diamond until someone tossed it aside. Most of us do not have the self-worth to yell, "Hey, that's the Hope diamond you just discussed!" But it might have been.

December 5

Help is all around us. Help is at every hand. Help is just waiting to meet and greet us. We are the ones who insist there is no help. Our hearts are closed to the many gentle forms of help that are offered to our suffering souls. What we are after, all that we need, is a sip of water. Our challenge is finding water when we are in a spiritual drought. We need the gentle drought of encouragement, the water of spiritual truth. "There is a God," we need to hear. "You are cared for," we need to believe.

December 6

To effect a creative recovery, we must undergo a time of mourning. In dealing with the suicide of the "nice" self we have been making do with, we find a certain amount of grief to be essential. Our tears prepare the ground for our future growth. Without this creative moistening, we may remain barren. We must allow the bolt of pain to strike us. Remember, this is useful pain; lightning illuminates.

December 7

As artists, we are open-minded but we need not be gullible. Many of the people purporting to be able to help us shape our craft have very little experience with crafting something themselves. What we are looking for is people who have done what we want to do—not someone who has watched others do it. It feels different to be in the cockpit at Cape Canaveral than it does to watch from the ground. As artists, we must find people who can share actual experience rather than a sanitized, dramatized, glorified, or press-filtered version. We must ask ourselves always, "Am I opening myself or my art to early and improper input, input that is ungrounded or inappropriate?" Another way to put it is: "Do they really know more about what I am doing than I do?"

December 8

For me to survive as a writer, there had better be a God, something larger and more powerful than *The New York Times*. Without such a God, I am lost. My career is hopeless, my dreams are futile, and I am helpless against the odds. With such a God, I just might have a chance. I need to carefully hoard my optimism. As artists we all need to believe we have a chance—because we do. I believe that the Great Creator loves other artists and is active on our behalf to find us a break. I believe this not only because I have to believe this, but also because it is my experience.

December 9

As your recovery progresses, you will come to experience a more comfortable faith in your creator and your creator within. You will learn that it is actually easier to write than not write, paint than not paint, and so forth. You will learn to enjoy the process of being a creative channel and to surrender your need to control the result. You will discover the joy of *practicing* your creativity. The process, not the product, will become your focus.

December 10

In recovering from our creative blocks, it is necessary to go gently and slowly. What we are after here is the healing of old wounds—not the creation of new ones. No high jumping, please! Mistakes are necessary! Stumbles are normal. Remember that in order to recover as an artist, you must be willing to be a bad artist. Give yourself permission to be a beginner. By being willing to be a bad artist, you have a chance to *be* an artist, and perhaps, over time, a very good one. Progress, not perfection, is what we should be asking of ourselves.

December 11

Optimism is an elected attitude, a form of emotional courage. It is a habit that can and must be learned if we are to survive as artists. So often, "things" look so bleak. In order to survive disappointments, we must master optimism, not as a form of denial but as a deeply rooted faith that we are somehow partnered in ways that we cannot see. We must look for the silver lining, knowing that there *always* is one.

December 12

It is difficult to commit to living where we are, how we are. It is difficult and it is necessary. In order to make art, we must first make an artful life, a life rich enough and diverse enough to give us fuel. We must strive to see the beauty in where we are planted, even if we are planted somewhere that feels very foreign to our own nature.

December 13

On a very primal level, writing is naughty. It is an act of self-possession. "This is what I think . . ." There is an anarchistic two-year-old inside most of us, and that child likes to have its say. When we let writing be about that, when we think of it as sharing secrets with ourselves, gleeful at what we are daring to do, writing doesn't take much "discipline."

December 14

When we admit that we love something or somebody, we are also loving ourselves. We are affirming, "It is I who love this." The "I" is also the "eye." Part of having a creative vision is allowing ourselves to see what we love. By celebrating what we love in this manner, we never have an unrequited love. Love becomes its own reward. What I love in you is the me that I find in you and the you that I find in me. I would say, if you want to be an artist, be a lover.

December 15

As an artist, so much of my life is determined by the size of my imagination. If I am making something big, and making it daily, I can perhaps live somewhere small. I can sit at a desk that faces a wall and tap words into space and my world is still large enough. I am more than my circumstances, more than the cage of my environment. There is a dignity inherent in making art, a filament of largesse and generosity, a connection to something better and brighter than myself. "You do not own me," I am able to say to the walls that enclose me. And yet, I must learn to love my walls.

December 16

Finding it hard to begin a project does not mean you will not be able to do it. It means you will need help—from your higher power, from supportive friends, and from yourself. First of all, you must give yourself permission to begin small and go in baby steps. These steps must be rewarded. Setting impossible goals creates enormous fear, which creates procrastination, which we wrongly call laziness. *Do not call procrastination laziness. Call it fear.* Fear is what blocks an artist. The fear of not being good enough. The fear of not finishing. The fear of failure and of success. The fear of beginning at all. There is only one cure for fear. That cure is love. *Use love for your artist to cure its fear.* Stop yelling at yourself. Be nice. Call fear by its right name.

December 17

Nobody wakes up to suddenly find themselves a best-selling author, a Tony Award–winning director, a Pulitzer Prize–winning playwright. Successful careers in the arts develop one step at a time. Books are written a page at a time. So are plays. A songwriting career unfolds song by song. An acting career involves each day's immersion in that craft. When we keep our sights trained on the small and doable, we are able to do the large and unthinkable. It is all a matter of breaking things down to a day-by-day practice: What can I manage today?

December 18

Silence is how we catch our breath. Silence is how we hear ourselves think, and also how we can hear the still, small voice speaking within us. As creative beings, we need silence. We need it or we create chaotic art rooted only in the reflection of what is around us, ungrounded in the deeper earth of ourselves.

December 19

When we remember that we are partnered, an ease enters our work. We begin to write more freely. We begin to paint with an inspired brush. Something or Someone larger than ourselves is striving to enter the world through us. We are the portal, the entryway, the gate. Through us great things come to pass. We are the conduits of a higher will. We are "humble" in the words of Piet Mondrian, essentially a "channel." When we cooperate, we feel a sense of right action, an ease. Cooperating with a Higher Power, rather than striving to conquer, we find ourselves carried along by the tide of what we are creating. There is an energy flow that moves us forward. There is a propulsion to what it is we would create. We open our hearts to what wishes to be born. We are receptive and what we receive is miraculous.

December 20

The long practice of daily work gives us the muscles and sinews to uphold the work that wants to move through us. The dancer's leg is trained not to quaver. So, too, we are trained as writers not to waver in the act of listening. By listening to what it is we are meant to write on a daily basis, we learn to let our writing write through us. A writing voice is not a collection of ticks and tricks. A writing voice is a vehicle for communication. The individuality of a voice emerges not by falling in love with your own facility but by learning to move past it.

December 21

A competitive focus encourages snap judgments: thumbs up or thumbs down. Does this project deserve to live? This is an indignity we offer our brain-children as they rear their heads in our consciousness. We judge them like beauty-pageant contestants. In a glance we may cut them down. We forget that not all babies are born beautiful, and so we abort the lives of awkward or unseemly projects that may be our finest work, our best creative ugly ducklings. An act of art needs time to mature. Never, ever, judge a fledgling piece of work too quickly. Be willing to paint or write badly while your ego yelps resistance. We must learn to approve of ourselves. Showing up for the work is the win that matters.

December 22

Help me to become more teachable. Help me to become more open. Help me to see your face in every face; your hand in every hand. Give me a child's delight in the world that you have fashioned. Help me to know that I can work with you and play with you to fashion the world still further. Give me a sense of your power and your majesty. Give me a graceful heart that acknowledges the Great Maker in all that has been made. Help me to know that I am an artist companioned by the Great Artist. Allow me to make my inventions as part of a greater whole. Help me to make all days, good days. Help me to create knowing that in fact I cocreate. Help me to be small that I may be a part of Something very large. Help me to revel in life's God-made delight.

December 23

As artists, we do well to practice consistency. Our mad dashes of inspiration leave us frustrated and at our wits' end. There is much to be said for a slower and more leisurely pursuit of ideas. There is so much talk of creative "breakthroughs" that many of us expect our creativity to be dramatic. This is seldom the case. Very occasionally, we will have a flash of insight or intuition but more often we will experience a slow and steady course. Our creativity resembles sunlight more than lightning. Even in dark times, this is true.

December 24

Blocked creatives like to think they are looking at changing their whole life in one fell swoop. This form of grandiosity is very often its own undoing. By setting the jumps too high and making the price tag too great, the recovering artist sets defeat in motion. Creative people are dramatic, and we use negative drama to scare ourselves out of our creativity with this notion of whole-sale and often destructive change. Fantasizing about pursuing our art full-time, we fail to pursue it part-time—or at all. Indulging ourselves in a frantic fantasy of what our life would look like if we were *real* artists, we fail to see the many small creative changes that we could make at this very moment. This kind of look-at-the-big-picture thinking ignores the fact that a creative life is grounded on many, many small steps and very, very few large leaps.

December 25

When artists are working regularly, they are spiritually centered. The act of making art is a spiritual act and our daily exposure to this realm does have an impact on our personality. It does not matter what language we use to describe it. Art puts us in touch with a power greater than ourselves. This conscious contact brings us a sense of optimism and grace. As we sense that there is a benevolent Something inclined toward helping us and our work, we begin to feel a sense of companionship. Higher forces are at our side. We are not alone.

December 26

Artists of all stripes tend to equate difficulty with virtue and ease with slumming. We do not lean into our ease and enjoy the ride of our gift. Instead, we make firm resolves to work on our areas of difficulty. We call this improving ourselves—okay, sometimes we do improve a wobbly area, but if we do not practice the joy of using our talents where they fall easily, we rob ourselves of self-expression. The "self" has a few things it "selfishly" enjoys—and it is dangerous, as an artist, to ignore these natural affections and predilections.

December 27

One of the most medicinal tasks we can undertake is a simple walk. It is difficult to remain mired in negativity and depression when we are "shaking it out" a little. Walking with an eye to the positive can take a gentle vigilance. As a form of medicine for ourselves, we can consciously turn our thoughts to the ancient practice of practicing gratitude—a footfall at a time. Take yourself out-of-doors and set a goal of a simple twenty-minute walk. Aiming toward the outer world, allow your inner world to fall into a brighter perspective by consciously—and concretely—enumerating your life's blessings. People, events, situations—any of these may be cause for gratitude. As you warm to your task of focusing on the good in your life, both your heart and your step will lighten.

December 28

One of the most difficult tasks an artist must face is a primal one: artistic survival. All artists must learn the art of surviving loss: Loss of hope, loss of face, loss of money, loss of self-belief. In addition to our many gains, we inevitably suffer these losses in an artistic career. They are the hazards of the road and, in many ways, its signposts. Artistic losses can be turned into artistic gains and strengths—but not in the isolation of the beleaguered artist's brain. In order to move through loss and beyond it, we must acknowledge it and share it. We must be alert to flag and mourn our losses.

December 29

Practicing our creativity is healing. Not because we are sick but because we are essentially well. As we express our intrinsic nature, which is beautiful and specific, particular and original, we experience a healing transformation less in ourselves than in our relationship to the world. We are not at fault. We are not powerless. We are very large, and in expressing this truth, healing occurs. What is healed is the rift between our spiritual stature and our mistaken perception of ourselves as flawed. Creativity is medicine. It is not dangerous or egotistical. It is life-affirming and essential. The more we use it, the more steadily and readily and easily we use it. The more we ground it and regularly access it, the better off we are. The "healthier" we are. Humor and acceptance enter the picture. Far more than self-scrutiny or self-correction, self-expression may be the key to a much more synthesized and effective sense of self.

December 30

Over any extended period of time, being an artist requires enthusiasm more than discipline. Enthusiasm is not an emotional state. It is a spiritual commitment, a loving surrender to our creative process, a loving recognition of all the creativity around us. Enthusiasm (from the Greek, "filled with God") is an ongoing energy supply tapped into the flow of life itself. Enthusiasm is grounded in play, not work. Far from being a brain-numbed soldier, our artist is actually our child within, our inner playmate. As with all playmates, it is joy, not duty, that makes for a lasting bond.

December 31

When we say that making art is an act of faith and that as we make art we pursue a spiritual path, we are not talking loosely. There is grace in our every artistic encounter. Miracles do happen. We do not plan them. We hope for them and then we are open to the creator's mentoring hand in improving our suggestions. What looks difficult or impossible to us does not appear difficult or impossible to the Great Creator. As we set our egos aside and allow that creative power to work through us, miracles are routinely accomplished—seemingly by our own hand. Creative energy is like electricity. It will flow whether we allow it to or not. The minute we relinquish the notion that our creative dreams are centered in the ego, the minute we begin to see them as spiritual adventures, we allow the Great Creator to shape us as only it can and will.

Sources

Selections from *The Artist's Way*,
Walking in This World, and
Finding Water are taken from
The Complete Artist's Way.

January 1; *The Artist's Way*,
pp. 153–54

January 2; *The Artist's Way*, p. 29

January 3; *The Artist's Way*, p. 117

January 4; *The Artist's Way*, p. 85

January 5; *The Artist's Way*, p. 33

January 6; *The Artist's Way*, p. 144

January 7; *The Artist's Way*, p. 14

January 8; *Walking in This World*,
pp. 319–20

January 9; *The Right to Write*, p. 79

January 10; *The Artist's Way*,
p. 101

January 11; *The Artist's Way*,
p. 106

January 12; *The Artist's Way*, p. 26

January 13; *The Right to Write*, p. 3

January 14; *The Artist's Way*,
p. 75

January 15; *The Right to Write*,
p. 105

January 16; *The Artist's Way*,
p. 158

January 17; *The Artist's Way*, p. 13

January 18; *The Right to Write*,
p. 101

January 19; *The Artist's Way*,
pp. 186–87

January 20; *Finding Water*, p. 689

January 21; *The Right to Write*,
pp. 15–16

May 13; *Walking in This World,*
p. 263

May 14; *The Artist's Way,* p. 116

May 15; *Walking in This World,*
p. 407

May 16; *The Artist's Way,* p. 96

May 17; *Finding Water,* p. 660

May 18; *Finding Water,* pp. 590–91

May 19; *The Right to Write,* p. 13

May 20; *The Sound of Paper,* p. 34

May 21; *The Right to Write,* p. 94

May 22; *The Artist's Way,*
pp. 45–46

May 23; *The Sound of Paper,* p. 35

May 24; *The Sound of Paper,* p. 137

May 25; *The Right to Write,* p. 1

May 26; *The Vein of Gold,* p. 4

May 27; *The Sound of Paper,* p. 49

May 28; *Finding Water,* p. 591

May 29; *The Sound of Paper,* p. 144

May 30; *The Sound of Paper,* p. 97

May 31; *The Vein of Gold,* p. 128

June 1; *The Artist's Way,*
pp. 194–95

June 2; *The Right to Write,*
pp. 206–7

June 3; *The Artist's Way,*
pp. 118–19

June 4; *The Sound of Paper,* p. 160

June 5; *The Right to Write,* p. 38

June 6; *The Sound of Paper,* p. 165

June 7; *Finding Water,* p. 596

June 8; *The Vein of Gold,* p. 191

June 9; *The Right to Write,* p. 31

June 10; *The Sound of Paper,*
pp. 154–55

June 11; *The Vein of Gold,* p. 189

June 12; *Walking in This World,*
pp. 283–84

June 13; *The Right to Write,* p. 155

June 14; *Walking in This World,*
p. 344

June 15; *Finding Water,* p. 644

June 16; *The Artist's Way,* p. 145

June 17; *Finding Water,* p. 664

June 18; *The Artist's Way,*
pp. 27–28

June 19; *Walking in This World,*
p. 242

June 20; *The Artist's Way,* p. 131

June 21; *The Artist's Way,* p. 56

June 22; *Walking in This World,*
p. 285

June 23; *The Sound of Paper,* p. 51

June 24; *The Artist's Way,*
pp. 17–18

June 25; *The Vein of Gold,* p. 138

June 26; *The Right to Write,* p. 152

June 27; *The Vein of Gold,* p. 139

June 28; *The Artist's Way*,
pp. 168–69

June 29; *Walking in This World*,
p. 340

June 30; *Walking in This World*,
p. 415

July 1; *Walking in This World*,
p. 248

July 2; *Finding Water*, p. 604

July 3; *The Right to Write*, p. 18

July 4; *Walking in This World*,
p. 313

July 5; *The Artist's Way*, p. 138

July 6; *The Right to Write*, p. 212

July 7; *The Sound of Paper*, p. 121

July 8; *The Vein of Gold*, p. 146

July 9; *The Sound of Paper*, p. 98

July 10; *The Vein of Gold*,
pp. 277–78

July 11; *The Right to Write*, p. 218

July 12; *The Sound of Paper*, p. 123

July 13; *The Vein of Gold*, p. 147

July 14; *Walking in This World*,
pp. 410–11

July 15; *The Sound of Paper*, p. 105

July 16; *The Right to Write*,
pp. 218–19

July 17; *Walking in This World*,
pp. 315, 317–18

July 18; *Walking in This World*,
p. 355

July 19; *Finding Water*, p. 556

July 20; *The Sound of Paper*, p. 54

July 21; *The Vein of Gold*, p. 287

July 22; *Walking in This World*,
p. 243

July 23; *The Vein of Gold*, p. 300

July 24; *The Sound of Paper*, p. 8

July 25; *The Artist's Way*,
pp. 46–47

July 26; *The Vein of Gold*, p. 37

July 27; *The Right to Write*, p. 220

July 28; *Walking in This World*,
p. 359

July 29; *The Sound of Paper*, p. 112

July 30; *Walking in This World*,
p. 279

July 31; *The Right to Write*, p. 66

August 1; *Finding Water*, p. 574

August 2; *The Right to Write*, p. 52

August 3; *The Sound of Paper*,
p. 263

August 4; *The Right to Write*,
p. 223

August 5; *The Sound of Paper*,
p. 62

August 6; *Walking in This World*,
pp. 456–57

September 10; *The Artist's Way*, p. 18

September 11; *Walking in This World*, p. 295

September 12; *Walking in This World*, p. 360

September 13; *Walking in This World*, p. 277

September 14; *The Right to Write*, p. 100

September 15; *Walking in This World*, p. 322

September 16; *The Right to Write*, p. 173

September 17; *Finding Water*, p. 704

September 18; *The Artist's Way*, p. 102

September 19; *The Right to Write*, p. 60

September 20; *Walking in This World*, pp. 372–73

September 21; *Finding Water*, p. 662

September 22; *Walking in This World*, p. 323

September 23; *Walking in This World*, p. 421

September 24; *The Artist's Way*, pp. 44–45

September 25; *The Right to Write*, p. 8

September 26; *The Artist's Way*, p. 179

September 27; *Finding Water*, p. 637

September 28; *The Right to Write*, p. 83

September 29; *Finding Water*, pp. 639–40

September 30; *Walking in This World*, p. 287

October 1; *The Right to Write*, 172

October 2; *Finding Water*, pp. 524–25

October 3; *The Artist's Way*, pp. 104–05

October 4; *The Right to Write*, p. 224

October 5; *The Right to Write*, p. 94

October 6; *The Artist's Way*, p. 23

October 7; *Finding Water*, p. 677

October 8; *Finding Water*, p. 644

October 9; *The Artist's Way*, pp. 170–71

October 10; *The Artist's Way*, pp. 171–72

October 11; *The Artist's Way*, p. 66

©Aloma

To order call 1-800-788-6262 or visit our website at www.penguin.com.

ABOUT THE AUTHOR

Julia Cameron has been an active artist for more than thirty years. She is the author of thirty-three books, fiction and non-fiction, including her bestselling works on the creative process: *The Artist's Way*, *Walking in This World*, *Finding Water*, *The Writing Diet*, *The Right to Write*, and *The Sound of Paper*. A novelist, playwright, songwriter, and poet, she has multiple credits in theater, film, and television.